MIRACLE IN KIGALI

The Rwandan Genocide – a survivor's journey

To John and Calnie
you will always be in my heart

MIRACLE IN KIGALI

The Rwandan Genocide
– a survivor's journey

Illuminée Nganemariya
with Paul Dickson

Miracle in Kigali

Miracle in Kigali 2019 edition published by Paul Dickson Books, April 2019.

Paul Dickson Books, 8 Bridge Court, Fishergate, Norwich NR3 1UE
t. 01603 666011, e. paul@pauldicksonbooks.co.uk www.pauldicksonbooks.co.uk

Miracle in Kigali was first published in Great Britain by The Tagman Press in 2007, with subsequent editions in 2008 and 2010 and an e-book edition in 2012.

ISBN
Paperback 978-0-9956187-9-4
E-book 978-1-9160550-0-1

A CIP catalogue record for this book is available from the British Library

2007 edition edited by Caroline Merz
2019 edition edited by Paul Dickson

2007, 2008 and 2010 editions text and cover design: Tessa Johnson, Richard Legg and Brendan Rallison
2019 edition text and cover design: Brendan Rallison

Illuminée and Roger cover photograph: Paul Dickson

Printed by Interprint in Norwich

Contents

Photographs between pages 88 and 89

- ID Card photograph of Dad, showing damage to his face following Calixte's attack *(Chapter two: Love thy neighbour)*.
- Me, aged three with my best friend, Eustache.
- Mum and Dad in our backyard in the early 1970s.
- John and me at home planning our wedding. This is the only photograph that I have of us together.
- Our wedding day, April 3, 1994. This is the only photograph that I have of our wedding. My sister Calnie is in the background holding a pitcher of banana beer.
- John photographed at Aunt Azera's house.
- Roger and me in 1995 with Steve from RTV Brussels. This was my first job after the Genocide. I worked as an interpreter.
- Cousin Esther and her daughter Babish with Mum and Roger (1995).
- Bosco, the man who saved me from the Interahamwe, after his return from Zaire and release from prison.
- With Roger outside our home in Bowthorpe, Norwich (1997).
- Roger playing for Heigham Park Rangers (October 2006).
- In London at the meeting with President Kagame (December 2006).
- With Shirley Timewell and Lester Tubby in the kitchen at Gt. Yarmouth College (February 2007).
- At work in the kitchen, Gt. Yarmouth College (February 2007)
- Roger, Paul and me – fundraising day for Rwandan orphans at Glynis Potter's Harambee shop (February 2007).
- Eustache, me and Drocelle (Kigali, October 2006).
- With Roger at Agakera National Park (October 2006).
- Berencille, Mum and Drocelle (March 2007).
- Eustache with his children: back, Moiise and Mandela and front, Benita, Benjamin and Gisa (March 2007).
- Eustache, Roger and me at the *Miracle in Kigali* launch, Sainsbury Centre for Visual Arts, Norwich, October 2007. Photograph, Norman Pierpoint.
- Paul, me and Tony Grey at Great Yarmouth College, November 2007. Photograph, Norman Pierpoint.
- Paul and me at the Rwandan launch, Hotel des Mille Collines, Kigali, July 2008.
- Book signing at the Rwandan launch, Hotel des Mille Collines, Kigali, July 2008.
- Paul's daughter, Rebecca, with my nephews Raymond and Claude and a huge bunch of green bananas, Rwanda July 2008.

- Me with the Macmillan team at the British Embassy, Kigali, July 2008
- Me with Rev'd Norman Steer at 50 Christmas Trees in a Church, Dickleburgh, Norfolk, December 2009.
- Roger on the *Africa United* set, Ruhengeri, Rwanda 2010. Photograph Nick Wall © Pathé Productions, British Broadcasting Corporation, UK Film Council, Africa United Limited, Dudu Productions Limited and Manbury Trading (Propietary) Limited 2010.
- On the red carpet at the Africa United premiere, Odeon, Leicester Square, London, October 2010.
- Fiona Rawlinson and me at St Peter and St James Church, Hereford, November 2011.
- Roger as Jumah in *Sixteen.* Photograph © Seize Films.
- Roger at the RTS West of England Awards evening, March 2017. Rob Brown, *Sixteen's* Director, is holding the trophy.
- Les Blancs, National Theatre, programme cover
- Roger as Dadir Hassan in BBC drama, Informer. Photograph © Neal Street Productions/BBC
- Roger and me with Stephen Bumfrey after an interview on his BBC Radio Norfolk show, January 2019.

Foreword to the 2019 edition

Illuminée Nganemariya

This new edition of Miracle in Kigali has been published to mark the 25th anniversary of the Rwandan Genocide. It is also Roger's 25th birthday in May. He was born in the most stressful conditions imagineable, but is now making his way in the world as a man, pursuing an acting and directing career. I am so proud of what he has achieved and my fingers are firmly crossed for him to get many more exciting roles in TV and films, like Dadir Hassan in the BBC drama Informer, last autumn.

Every time I visit Rwanda, I am struck by the pace of change and the shared desire to become the most successful economy in East Africa. My nephews and nieces are growing up in a country that has changed immeasurably from the Rwanda of my childhood.

Never again is the mantra, and in April the country pauses for the Genocide commemoration, with the main events staged at the Amahoro Stadium in Kigali. Roger contributed to the commemoration in 2011, when the Roger: Genocide Baby documentary was being filmed.

We have staged Genocide commemorations in Norwich, attended by friends and members of the local community. But every year I always head for Norwich Cathedral's Bauchon Chapel to light candles and remember in the peace and quiet.

What happened during the Genocide will be with me for the rest of my life. It still haunts my dreams, has an ongoing impact on my health with post-traumatic stress disorder and makes it difficult for me to trust people.

But as the saying goes, life goes on, and life has gone on since this book was first published in 2007. Many positive things have happened, especially with Roger's career.

We will be donating £2 for every book sold to North Norfolk's Glaven Valley Churches, for their work in rural Rwanda through the Life in Abundance charity. Claude and Ethne Scott have written a piece about the Glaven Valley Churches' project, which we have included in the book as appendix four.

Thank you for buying Miracle in Kigali.

Illuminée Nganemariya
Norwich
March 2019

A message from His Excellency Claver Gatete, Ambassador of the Republic of Rwanda to the United Kingdom and the Republic of Ireland 2007 edition.

Illuminée Nganemariya's story is one of great courage in the face of the unimaginable horrors that beset our country in the spring of 1994.

Survivors of the Genocide who read this book will be able to connect with Illuminée's experiences. It will help them come to terms with the madness that gripped Rwanda and destroyed hundreds of thousands of lives.

Writing *Miracle in Kigali* has been an important part of Illuminée's therapy as she has struggled to come to terms with her own personal grief and loss. I hope that its publication will help her to look forward positively to the rest of her life.

It is important that we never forget what happened in Rwanda. *Miracle in Kigali* plays a role in healing the scars of the Genocide. But it is also a very useful contribution to bringing the events of 1994 to a worldwide audience.

My Government is determined to develop a bright future for Rwanda so that Rwandans, whether they live at home or in the Diaspora, like Illuminée and her son Roger, can be proud of their country and contribute to its recovery.

To my knowledge, *Miracle in Kigali* is the first book written by a Genocide survivor living in the United Kingdom. You have made a wise purchase. I hope this book inspires you to discover more about our beautiful land.

H.E. Claver Gatete
Ambassador
Embassy of Rwanda, London
May 2007
www.ambarwanda.org.uk

Foreword to 2007 edition

Illuminée Nganemariya

When I started writing this book I asked myself, 'What do I want to tell the people who are reading my story?' For Rwandan readers still living in Rwanda or born and living abroad, and British readers who do not understand the true story about what happened to my beautiful small country – I have written this book for you.

All over the world people have heard about Rwanda, but they have only heard bad things. They have heard about the hate, 'La Haine', between Rwandans. The focus of this book is my journey through the Genocide and beyond. And as you read about my experiences during the '100 days' you will be horrified by the casual way in which Rwandan murdered fellow Rwandan.

But 13 years after the Genocide, I also want you to take a message of hope for the future. This is a story that is known to all Rwandans. When a farmer wants a good harvest, first he checks his field to make sure that the earth is prepared, and removes all the weeds and stones. He looks for a weed we call urwili, which spreads very fast and takes a long time to remove. Then he sows the seed. He continuously checks the crop to make sure it is growing well, is not diseased and is free of weeds. If he does this he is sure to get a good crop, because in Rwanda we have wonderful weather. It is always good!

But I think that in Rwanda, the weed is still there. We still have a problem that we have not resolved. Museveni, the President of our neighbouring country, Uganda, thinks the same way. He visited Rwanda after the Genocide and said that most Rwandans have a parasitic insect that lives in their feet and hands. It has to be turned and twisted very carefully to get it out without leaving eggs in the body. By this he meant that Rwanda had a disease or problem, and that we would have to act with great care and thought. Some Rwandans thought he meant that Hutus were the disease, and that he meant to kill them. This was a completely incorrect interpretation of his story.

We Rwandans so often blame others for our problems – twitana bamwana, as we say. In French there is an expression 'qualitie et defaut', which means two things to all Rwandans. We think we know better than other people do and, if something bad happens, it is always someone else's fault. We never accept responsibility for the things that we do. But every Rwandan needs to accept that we have a problem in our country, and to take personal responsibility for trying to resolve it.

3

Fortunately Rwanda is gradually healing its wounds under the leader-ship of President Paul Kagame. The Genocide ripped apart Rwanda's economy and destroyed its moral soul. We still have a long way to go, but I hope this book plays a small part in that reconstruction process.

I want to thank the people of Britain who let me and my son, Roger into their country when I left Rwanda with my cousin Esther in 1996, and for accepting me as one of their own by granting us asylum and giving us permission to stay here.

When my cousin returned to Rwanda in 1997, Janet Dalgleish helped me with my application for asylum, and Eric Maple, vicar in Bowthorpe, Norwich, and my friends there helped me in the beginning. Then I turned to Norfolk Social Services for help as I was in a strange city with a two year-old child, no money and hardly any English. They have helped ever since. Annie Moseley, Rosemary Horner, Julie Neeson, Hazel Flavell and Elaine Doherty have all supported me in so many ways.

Steven Christianson, my therapist from Norfolk Mental Health Care Trust, Dr Barker, Dr Moser, Dr Spitz and Dr Few and many nurses and carers – too many to name – have all been critical to my survival. Without them I would not have been able to continue living.

I would also like to thank Adrian Galvin who spent many hours with me recording my story. These tape recordings were eventually to form the basis of this book.

Finally I would like to thank Paul Dickson, who responded to my appeal in the Norwich Evening News for a collaborator to help finish my story, and to Anthony Grey for making this book a reality.

Illuminée Nganemariya
Norwich, February 2007

Introduction to 2007 edition

Paul Dickson

Thirteen years ago Rwanda's Hutu 'Power' extremists attempted to wipe their Tutsi compatriots from the face of the earth. Any moderate Hutus who stood in their way were also engulfed in this holocaust.

Friend murdered friend, slashing and cutting with machetes and spears. 'Lucky' victims paid for a quicker despatch, courtesy of a bullet to the head. In little more than three months, from April 6 to July 4, 1994, some 800,000 people were murdered. The killing rate was faster than the Nazis achieved in their industrial gas chambers. The army and Interahamwe (meaning 'those who work together') militia recruited entire local communities to their cause, tracking down every last Tutsi. To refuse resulted in an immediate death sentence.

One of Africa's most beautiful and fertile countries, Le Pays des Mille Collines – land of a thousand hills – descended into unimaginable savagery. Western nations stood on the sidelines as Rwanda crumbled. The tiny United Nations force in Kigali, led by General Romeo Dallaire, was impotent. Despite Dallaire's urgent protests, his soldiers were not allowed to intervene.

The media reported tales of death and destruction. But this was Africa; they were always killing each other on the 'Dark Continent'. Readers turned the page and checked their share prices or the latest cricket scores.

But despite Western ambivalence, the 'Hutu Power' objective was thwarted. The Rwandan Patriotic Front (RPF) invaded from Uganda. This Tutsi-led exile army eventually stopped the mass slaughter, but sparked a Hutu exodus. Some two million Hutu fled to Zaire (now Democratic Republic of Congo) – and to disease and death on the plains of Goma. Spurred on by the Interahamwe, who told lurid stories of alleged RPF atrocities, whole villages abandoned their homes and farms.

It was only then that the West finally woke up to the tragedy of Rwanda. Too late for Tutsi women and children lost in the Genocide. Too late for Hutu women and children dying from cholera in the squalor of a Congolese refugee camp. But against all the odds, some innocent bystanders did survive. Swept along by the horrors of the Genocide and then spat out alive at its conclusion, how could these people ever make sense of their experiences and pick up the pieces of their broken lives?

This is the story of one such survivor. Illuminée Nganemariya was born in 1968 into a middle class Tutsi family. Her family had already suffered in the early Hutu reprisals. Relatives on both her father and mother's sides of the family had been murdered. But Illuminée had a happy and stable childhood with both Hutu and Tutsi friends. Her first brush with repression came at the age of 11 when she had to identify herself as a Tutsi at school, and subsequently 'failed' her exam for secondary school.

The growth of extreme 'Hutu Power' parties during the late 1980s and early 1990s had little impact on her day-to-day life. Tutsis, however, learned to stay indoors during local party meetings, when drunken sessions often ended in violence.

Illuminée met her husband John in 1993. He was the former husband of Illuminée's best friend, who had died in childbirth. When Illuminée realised she was pregnant, her family was horrified: she was a 'good Catholic girl'. Her pregnancy developed against a background of increasing tension. Tutsis disappeared overnight, and nobody was apprehended for their murder.

Eventually Illuminée's family agreed to her marriage with John, and everyone was reunited for a day of joy and happiness. On April 3, 1994, Hutu and Tutsi friends drank and celebrated together. Forty-eight hours later, Rwandan President Habyarimana was killed when his plane was shot down on the approach to Kigali airport. Habyarimana was on his way back from Arusha in Tanzania, where he had had a meeting with neighbouring heads of state.

The 'Hutu Power' extremists blamed Tutsis for the President's death. Radio Mille Collines, 'Hutu Power' radio, broadcast a steady stream of vitriol against Tutsis encouraging Hutus to rid Rwanda of the inyenzi (cockroaches), the Tutsis who threatened the future of the Hutus.

The Genocide began, and John and Illuminée's new life together became a casualty of the systematic extermination of Tutsis in their neighbourhood. Illuminée lost her husband of one month, killed in horrific circumstances by his Hutu friends.

Meanwhile their son Roger was born. Illuminée, expecting to die at any moment, embarked on an incredible journey of survival. Life was cheap, but Illuminée miraculously passed through the anarchic chaos of the '100 days' with her son, to face the trauma of post-Genocide Rwanda. She even joined the Hutu exodus to Zaire (now Democratic Republic of Congo), only to be turned back on the hills above Kigali by soldiers from the victorious RPF.

Delivered by the RPF from possible death on the plains of Goma, Illuminée's long struggle to come to terms with her experiences began. That process has been incredibly difficult. The Genocide will always be with her, a nightmare that can be vividly replayed, unlocked by the noise from a barrage of fireworks, gunshots on TV, a camera flash or even the sound of a car backfiring.

Although she is only 38, Illuminée says that she is 'old in her head'. The Genocide stole her youth. But Illuminée has a strong sense that she was spared for a reason: to tell her story and help people understand the impact of the Genocide on ordinary people. In this way she hopes to aid the process of reconciliation in Rwanda, where thousands of widows, widowers and orphans are still struggling with their own horror stories. Telling the story is also an important part of Illuminée's personal therapy, ensuring that what happened to her family is documented for Roger and for future generations.

I first met Illuminée and Roger in April 2006 when our local newspaper, the Norwich Evening News, featured an item about their lives as the only Rwandans in the city. It also included an appeal from Illuminée for someone to collaborate with her on a book.

I could so easily have turned the page, but something told me to pick up the phone. That speculative call opened a new chapter in my life and an intense desire to ensure that Illuminée's story was told.

This is the result.

Rwanda

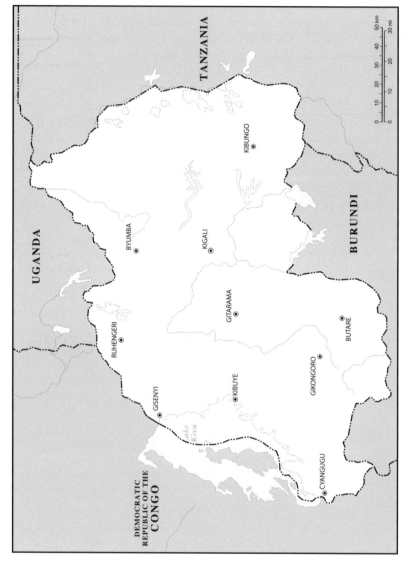

Chapter one

The Winds of Destruction

Animosity between Rwanda's Hutus and Tutsis grew significantly after the Belgian colonists arrived in 1916. The Belgians saw the two groups as distinct entities, and even produced identity cards classifying people according to their ethnicity. They considered the Tutsis superior to the Hutus, educating the former in Catholic schools and giving them better job opportunities. Resentment among the Hutus gradually built up, culminating in a series of riots in 1959. More than 20,000 Tutsis were killed, and many more fled to the neighbouring countries of Burundi, Tanzania and Uganda.

My dad, Etienne Karekezi, was born in 1916. He was from the Abagunga clan who originated in southern Rwanda. His father was a farmer who had lived in the Kigali area from the early years of the 20th century.

The Roman Catholic missionaries arrived in Rwanda in the wake of the Belgians, who had taken over from the Germans at the end of World War I. Most families refused to allow their children to be educated by the missionaries, but my grandparents agreed, so Dad went to the mission school. I am glad that they let him go, because Dad learnt how to read and write, as well as picking up French and Swahili to add to his native language, Kinyarwanda. He also converted to Roman Catholicism. Religion was a big part of his life. He was very devout and made sure that all his children were brought up in the faith.

By the time Dad was old enough to get a job, a lot of Europeans had arrived in the country. It was difficult for them to communicate with the Rwandese, but because he could speak French, he was well placed to interpret. Towards the end of the colonial period he worked for an Indian company that manufactured clothing.

My mum, Rosette Nyiragakwavu, was born around 1930. She came from a well-to-do family which had links to the Abatsobe clan from Gitarama and Butare. The Abatsobe was historically Rwanda's governing clan. Her father was a wealthy man with lots of cows and land.

My parents' marriage was arranged. Mum's cousin lived near Dad, and introduced them after his first wife died. However there were 'rumblings' in Mum's family about a poor Tutsi with no cows marrying her. We used to joke that Dad, the son of a farmer, had done well to marry such a well-connected woman! My father's first wife was a beauty called Mwambarakanda, who died young from a liver disease. She and Dad had three children. Mum was quite plain by comparison, but she was an intelligent woman who came from a well-educated family. Unfortunately the marriage was not well received by my Dad's family, who accused Mum of being bossy and controlling.

They married in the early 1950s and lived in a village – now a suburb of Kigali – called Gacuriro, to the north of the capital. Mum still lives in the village.

My eldest sister, Berencille Dedeli, was born in 1952. My parents then had two more daughters: Calnie Kaligirwa, born in 1954, and Drocelle Bazubagira, born in 1960. My brother, Eustache Twagirayezu, followed in 1964, and I was born in 1968.

Most of Mum's family was killed during the first reprisals against the Tutsis in 1959, known as The Winds of Destruction. Many of them lived near the River Nyabarongo and tried to swim across the water to get away from the Hutu killers. But they were followed into the water and were savagely stabbed with sharpened bamboo sticks until they died.

Mum has never really talked about this, although she did tell us about her uncle, Raphael Gakwaya. Raphael was savagely beaten by a Hutu mob. As he lay dying, he was asked by a priest, who was standing by watching what was going on, whether there was anything he wanted to say to cleanse his soul. Raphael refused to be blessed by a supposed holy man who was tacitly supporting the killers. He was a real hero to us all. Sadly the collusion of priests with the 1959 massacres was to be repeated with devastating effect in the 1994 Genocide.

Dad had four brothers. One left Rwanda in 1959, one died in prison and the other two died of natural causes. So my father became head of the family, and inherited a large amount of land.

During The Winds of Destruction, Tutsis sought sanctuary in their local church. Fortunately the Hutu priest who stood by and watched my uncle's death was an exception, and the church was a safe place to hide. So Dad, Mum, Berencille and Calnie stayed at their church until the killings stopped. My family also turned to the church for sanctuary during the widespread campaign against Tutsis in 1963. This followed the unsuccessful invasion of a Tutsi émigré army from Burundi.

Dad's house was destroyed by the Hutu mob in 1959, so he patiently rebuilt it and the family moved back home, hoping that life would get back to normal. But their hopes were soon to be dashed by a knock at the door.

Chapter two

Love thy neighbour

A referendum was held in 1960 to establish whether Rwanda should become a republic or remain a kingdom. The result showed overwhelming support for a republic. Grégoire Kayibanda, leader of the PARMEHUTU Party, became Rwanda's first elected president.

When Belgium relinquished power and granted Rwanda independence in 1962, power was firmly in the hands of the Hutus. From then on the Tutsis became the national scapegoats. The country's previous history under a Tutsi monarchy and then as a colony was rejected: the new Rwanda was to be Hutu and Catholic.

One evening, not long after the family had moved into their rebuilt home, there was a knock on the door. Mum went to see who it was. Calixte Ribakare, our Hutu neighbour, was there with a group of people from our community. He asked to see Dad. Mum said he was asleep, but they insisted that she wake him, as they wanted to talk. She did as they asked, but when Dad appeared Calixte and his friends attacked him with sticks and nails. They left him in a pool of blood and ran off into the night.

I think it was Dad's employment with a Belgian clothing company and perceived association with our colonial masters that singled him out for punishment in 1959, and led to the destruction of the house and Calixte's attack.

Mum took him to hospital. He was there for almost a year and lost one eye. The doctors gave him a glass eye, but he did not like it and wore dark glasses. The doctors said that he should not drink alcohol and that he should rest as much as possible. Rest was really out of the question, as he had a family to look after. He was also very fond of his banana beer, urwagwa. Rather than give up drinking, he used alcohol to help him get over the trauma of the attack and his year in hospital. In his youth, Dad had been an extremely handsome man, always well dressed and spoken. His disfigured features were to be a lasting reminder of what had happened in 1959.

When I was little, I used to ask him how he had lost his eye. He would tell me that a bird had taken it out. Mum eventually told me the full story, which I found very difficult to understand. Years later, it was almost impossible to believe what had passed between Calixte and my father. Dad seemed to go out of his way to be friendly to our grumpy Hutu neighbour. He would invite Calixte in for a drink and the two of them would chat for ages. Dad would often ask us to sweep Calixte's front garden or fetch water for him – not that we received any thanks for our efforts and neighbourly kindness. In fact Calixte would often shout at us if our chickens strayed into his garden.

But still Dad insisted on treating him well. He argued that Calixte had experienced many difficulties in his life; most of his children had died young and his wife was frequently ill. Even so, Dad's forgiveness seemed to be super-human, especially as he never really recovered from Calixte's beating. Others might have sought revenge, an eye for an eye. But Dad loved the neighbour who had left him for dead – beaten and half-blind on his doorstep.

For Dad it was important that 'La Haine', the hatred between Hutu and Tutsi, did not spread to the next generation. Nevertheless, it was sometimes very difficult for us, and Eustache would often storm out of the house when Calixte visited.

When Calixte was dying he relied on Dad more than ever. He was frightened, but my father talked calmly to him to give him reassurance. Dad was true to his Christian beliefs; no matter what had happened, he was there for his neighbour at the end.

Chapter three

Family life

The Hutu government set up a quota system under which Tutsis were allowed only ten per cent of school and university places, as well as civil service jobs. The government also continued the Belgian's policy of labelling people with ethnic identity cards.

Dad was a kind and sociable man and, like many Rwandans, had his own banana beer pit covered by leaves next to the house. Most of the beer was sold, but Dad and his friends and neighbours drank some of it. You did not even have to be an acquaintance to enjoy his hospitality – sometimes he would invite strangers passing the house to have a drink. When he had over indulged, Dad would start talking in French and sing religious songs. Sometimes he would forget where he had put his glasses and would crash around trying to find them, much to our amusement and Mum's annoyance!

She used to get cross when he had a house full of people drinking. But her concerns were as much for him as for herself. Dad had been advised not to drink by the doctors after Calixte's attack, and she was irritated that he chose to ignore that advice. Mum did not drink; she said it gave her headaches. Her attitude was that relaxation was the reward for hard work. But Mum never seemed to reward herself. What little spare time she had to herself – when she wasn't looking after the family, working in the fields or selling our produce at market – was spent making a basket or doing something practical.

Even when she finally found a moment to sit down, smoke her pipe and read Imvaho Kinyamateka, a Rwandan religious newspaper, she would do it in a planned way. I think she preferred work to talk, which was unusual for a Rwandan! Mum was not unfriendly or cold, but she set strict limits on time for chatting and socialising. She was not afraid to say, 'That's it. I have things to do.'

My parents lived with their differences and made a happy home for their family. If they did have loud arguments, they kept them well away from me. Divorce was extremely rare in Rwanda when I was growing up. When stress levels were high, the husband or wife would go back to live with their family for a week or so until things cooled off. I remember that Calnie moved in with us at one time, after her husband came out of prison following a round-up of young Tutsis suspected of having links with the RPF. He had been drinking heavily. But that never happened with Mum and Dad.

We were rarely beaten as children. Mum, with her quiet authority, did not need to use force and Dad was very easy-going most of the time.

As the youngest member of the family I was quite spoilt. I always felt at the centre of things. Mum breast-fed me until the age of five and, despite all kinds of threats, I would follow her round tugging at her clothes. In the end she put a stop to my constant demands by rubbing raw chillies on her nipples! Even so, I slept in my parents' bed until I was seven. This was very unusual in Rwanda. Dad, in particular, indulged me. I do not think he ever finished a plate of food when I was around – always saving the last mouthful for me.

Berencille, my oldest sister, was like Mum: tough, organised and always busy. If I lay in bed too long, she would haul off the sheets and cover me in cold water! With her around I did not get too much of a chance to be a princess. I had my chores like fetching the water before school in the morning, and Berencille always made sure that I did my homework.

I had to get up at 6am to carry out my water chore, but it was fun. I went to the well with my friends. I carried 12 litres on my head. It was a 90-minute round trip, so carrying it was quite hard work on the way back. Of course if I spilled the water I had to turn round and fill it up again. My brother and I could not carry all the water for the family's needs, so we also employed someone to collect additional supplies for the home and our crops.

There was more walking on the way to school – 30 minutes there and 30 minutes back. My first high school was even further away – 90 minutes there and 90 minutes back. Then when I came home from school, I had to fetch more water. Some children had to gather the wood as well, but we had someone who

15

did that for us. We also had a woman who helped Mum in the house. After we had been to get the evening water, Eustache and I were allowed to play with our friends. When we came home, we always had a shower – not like a shower in Britain, but a big bowl of water which we splashed all over our bodies. It was great to cool down after playing.

We had our tea together at about 7pm. Children sat on a mat on the floor. We mainly used our hands – no knives and forks – but our hands were always washed and clean!

Because Dad was very religious, we prayed together in the morning, before meals and before we went to bed. We also went to church every Sunday. I had inherited Dad's love of religion, and my bedroom became a shrine to the Virgin Mary. Well into my teenage years I was convinced that I would become a nun.

When Dad had drunk his banana beer, he would often sing religious songs. I really enjoyed singing with him. We always had a special singing session on Christmas Eve. This was a lovely family time.

There is no tradition in Rwanda of giving presents at Christmas or on birthdays. The only time that you get presents is when you get married. As a child I never knew what presents were, not like in the UK! But it was good, because nobody thought about presents. It was a much simpler, far less commercial life. We used to get involved in the religious festivals and, of course, we were baptised and made our First Communion. This occasion was the only time, apart from your wedding day, that you were given a present by your godparents. It was usually money – the equivalent of 20p – or something similar. But I remember feeling very happy because I had a nice white dress and shoes.

Lots of people still followed the old traditional religions, but I was never allowed to see the ceremonies. People would run around the village naked and sing loud songs together.

Calnie was outgoing, independent and physically brave. It was Calnie on whom we relied when we wanted a chicken for supper. Eustache and I were sent to corner a bird, which could take anything up to 30 minutes. Once captured, the victim would be handed to Calnie, who performed her duty expertly with a quick twist of the bird's neck. Not even Mum could do this.

Calnie was given the chance to go to a Government boarding school, thanks to my cousin, Arhanase Kayigamba, who was friendly with the Minister of Education. Succeeding Hutu Governments made it more and more difficult for Tutsi children to have a secondary education. Calnie was lucky, but she did not stay in the school for long, as she was caught up in an outbreak of violence against Tutsi students in 1973. This particular 'problem' was the Government's response to the murder of 150,000 Hutus by the Tutsi government in Burundi. President Kayibanda's regime in Rwanda launched a clampdown on the quota of Tutsis in education and the civil service. Calnie survived and left Rwanda for Zaire (Democratic Republic of Congo). It was a very brave thing to do, particularly as she was only 19. In Zaire she managed to get a job, which helped pay for her education. She eventually returned to Rwanda to launch a career as a teacher.

One of my earliest memories is of the 1973 troubles. A local Hutu teacher called Zingiro Augista came to our house one evening. He was making a register of all Tutsis in the village. All I was worried about was my stomach! I shouted at Mum and Berencille, saying 'You never give me anything to eat.' They ignored me and were very angry after Zingiro left. Mum said, 'How can you think about eating, when we are worried about what is going to happen?' Fortunately there was no violence in our village, and life soon returned to normal.

Sister number three, Drocelle, was different again. She was more like Dad, sharing his love of dancing. She always seemed to be happiest at a wedding or party. Even though I was the baby of the family, it was Drocelle who radiated carefree youthfulness, which lasted long beyond her teenage years. Drocelle finally married after the Genocide. She had four children and pretty much allowed them to do as they pleased. But her easy-going nature was combined with a very blunt tongue, and she was the most outspoken member of our family.

Poor Drocelle had a stomach complaint when she was growing up. We had a cousin called Josephine on my mother's side of the family who was a nurse. She offered to look after Drocelle, so she left home at the age of seven, (in 1967) and did not live permanently with us again until after the Genocide. I only really saw Drocelle at weekends. She was almost a stranger in my early years, but we gradually developed a relationship. I used to hate it when she left on Sunday evening and wondered why she did not live with us, as she often seemed to be very well.

Josephine's daughter, Esperance, two years my junior, was my best female friend when I was growing up. She would regularly stay with us. We had great fun fetching the water and generally got on well together. I was also very close to my niece Brigitte. She was my half brother Kayitani's daughter, but was only one year younger than me. Josephine was married to a wealthy Hutu from Kibuye called Jerome Muziganyi. He was a director of the government publishing company, and also owned a string of bars. He even managed to get Drocelle special medical treatment from the Minister of Health, who was a practising doctor from Kibuye. All in all Drocelle had quite a privileged existence in Jerome's household. I am sure that Mum and Dad knew that she was better off with Jerome and Josephine.

My brother Eustache was, and still is, my best friend. As he was a boy and five years my senior, he would often show his affection by teasing me, or playing practical jokes. He would say that I was a foundling and that I did not look like the rest of the family – which was only partly true. Or he would tell me that a wolf lived in my aunt's banana plantation and that whenever I passed through, I had to sing a marching song, or risk being eaten alive! I, of course, faithfully obeyed his instructions.

It was only after Eustache left home to go to the Red Cross mission school in Kacyiru, a distant Kigali suburb, that I realised how special he was to me and I was to him. On his return, Eustache would always make a fuss and give me presents of clothes or shoes. His character was a combination of Mum and Dad. He was kind like Dad, but also carried Mum's serious natural authority. I was proud to call him my brother.

Because Dad inherited all the family land from his brothers, we grew large crops of green bananas, sogum, sweet potatoes, beans, peanuts, cassava and sweet corn. Sogum is like wheat. It can be used to make porridge, a type of bread and even an alcoholic drink. It is a staple part of the Rwandan diet. In the back yard we grew onions and other vegetables, as well as rearing chickens. Most Rwandan people do not eat much meat. We had our chickens, but as we had no cows, Mum occasionally bought beef at the local market along with sugar, milk, oil, salt and rice.

Casual labourers worked on the land throughout the year. We would help during the school holidays. But at harvest time, all our friends and neighbours worked with us, Hutus and Tutsis together. Mum would cook lots of food and provided plenty to drink. It was a very happy time. I used to really enjoy getting involved and doing my bit for the harvest. Some of the surplus produce from the harvest was sold to our neighbours, and Mum went to the market to sell the rest.

During my early childhood I had no awareness of the difference between Hutu and Tutsi. I had lots of Hutu friends and lived in a very happy family. It was only when I tried to progress from primary to secondary education that I was made aware that I was different.

Chapter four

Hands up if you are a Tutsi

Tensions between Hutus and Tutsis remained high following independence. In 1972, some 150,000 Hutus were massacred in neighbouring Burundi. In the aftershock of the incident, Prime Minister Kayibanda was overthrown by his army commander, Major General Juvenal Habyarimana. In 1974, Habyarimana formed the Mouvement Républicain National pour le Développement (MRND).

For the next few years there was relative stability, but the economic situation worsened and, after nearly two decades in power, Habyarimana began losing popularity. In 1990 Rwanda was invaded by around 5000 well-armed Tutsi exiles, supported by some moderate Hutus – collectively called the Rwandan Patriotic Front (RPF) – from their base in Uganda, led by former Ugandan Army Commander-in-Chief, Major-General Fred Rwigyema, who was killed in early exchanges.

The Government's response to the invasion was to round up prominent Tutsis and anti-MRND Hutus who were imprisoned in barbaric conditions.

Meanwhile the RPF, now led by Paul Kagame, continued to mount a guerrilla campaign, boosted by a steady flow of young Tutsis and Hutus disillusioned with Habyarimana's government. The rural Hutu population, however, never greeted the rebels as conquering heroes. Thousands fled from border villages, creating a large internal refugee problem. At the same time, Hutu extremists embarked on regular killings of small groups of Tutsis, particularly in the Gisenyi and Ruhengeri Hutu heartland.

I really enjoyed life at primary school. Not everyone had the chance to go to school, because parents had to pay. I was very lucky, many girls had no education at all, as families' priority was normally to send boys to school. Fortunately it is much easier to get a basic education in Rwanda now, as President Kagame's government has introduced free education for primary school children. In my day, girls had two years of 'vocational' study at the end of their primary school time. We learnt how to sew and cook, along with other skills that would help us bring up a family. Girls were not supposed to aspire to further education and a career.

The first time that I realised that I was different was just before I took my exam for government high school. All Tutsis had to put their hands up to identify themselves and, of course, the rest of the class looked at us. It was very embarrassing. I realised that I was in a minority, and at the same time I was made to think that I had done something wrong. I also had to put my ethnic origin on the exam paper.

I failed the exam. This was no surprise, as Tutsi children normally failed their exams. I think they probably put my papers straight into the bin!

So I left primary school and embarked on a very lengthy secondary education. Dad paid for me to go to an exclusive Tutsi-run school called Apacope College. I had to sit a special entrance exam and did well, especially in arithmetic and languages. Most students were from rich families and, as a 'country' girl I did not fit in. My exam marks deteriorated, and after three years my parents decided that I should leave.

By now I was 17. I went to Ajesco College, where my performance improved, but sadly the Government closed it down after a year. But Dad decided to reward me for the improvement, and sent me back to Apacope College.

I thought that as I had completed four years of secondary education, they would put me into year five. But instead I was backtracked to the start of year four. This was not at all satisfactory, so at the end of the year Dad moved me once again and I went to Apace College, which was run by Seventh Day Adventists. It was very different going to a religious foundation, but at least I finally managed to get to the end of year five. By now I should have finished high school!

It was during my time at Apace College that I met John. He was very keen for me to finish my education, but of course that never happened thanks to the

Genocide. But more of John later. I would probably have pursued a career in accountancy if my life had been allowed to take its normal course.

My only work experience before the Genocide was a summer job with Oxfam, helping out at a camp near Kigali for refugees from Uganda. Esther, another cousin on my mum's side of the family, was the local director of Oxfam. Knowing someone who worked for an organisation was always the best way to get a job in Rwanda – and probably still is.

It was very difficult for Tutsis to get Government jobs, so most young men set up their own businesses. That was the best way for them to progress. Lots of grocery and clothes businesses were run by young Tutsis, especially in Kigali city centre. Successful Tutsi businessmen often attracted unwanted attention from the Government. They would travel on business to Uganda, Tanzania and Burundi, and had contact with émigré Tutsis who had fled during The Winds of Destruction and subsequent troubles. When the RPF invaded from Uganda in 1990, the Habyarimana regime put a lot of Tutsi businessmen in prison, accusing them of being spies and supporters of the Tutsi rebels.

Calnie's husband, a teacher called Jean Bosco Ntidendereza, was arrested in 1990. Lots of people died in prison and others died soon after they were released. I think the authorities must have poisoned them. Jean Bosco survived, but came out of prison a broken man and took to drinking heavily. Sadly he was a marked man. He gradually recovered from the trauma of prison, only to be murdered very early in the Genocide.

My teenage years were very sheltered, as Mum and Dad were protective. I always had to be home in the evening unless I had permission to go out, and I was never allowed out by myself. But there was good reason for this protectiveness in the Rwanda of the late 1980s and early 1990s, with the growth of extremist Hutu political parties and the establishment of the governing MRND party's Interahamwe militia. There were regular casual Tutsi killings and, as a result, Mum and Dad were concerned for the safety of their youngest child.

I had male and female friends during my high school years, but never a 'boyfriend'. This is probably one of the reasons why I did not fit in at Apacope College. All the wealthy Tutsi girls flaunted their boyfriends. I suppose this shy and religious girl from a village outside Kigali seemed odd to them. I was not, to use a British phrase, a party animal. I did not go to dances. I did not drink. One of my teachers had been very friendly, but I found it very difficult to explain my feelings to him, and also to tell my parents what was going on in my heart. So I just stayed at home and lived a quiet family life.

When I was about 15, I began taking responsibility for doing the family's washing. This was a very traditional task. Washing machines were unheard of in Rwanda. It was not until I came to Norwich that I grappled with my first 'automatic'. I carried all the washing on my head, wrapped up in a sheet, down to our local river, the Rwabana. It took 15 minutes to get there. Armed with a hard block of Surfo or Makasi soap, I washed the clothes by hand in the water and laid them on the grass to dry in the sun.

Occasionally I would have the luxury of a box of washing powder, which would make the job easier. Doing the washing was a full day's job. I spent most Saturdays down by the river, but it was very sociable as our neighbours would all be there too. However washing could at times be quite a stressful experience for me, as I was terrified of our large caterpillar, ikinyabwoya, which lurked in the long grass. The ikinyabwoyi latched on to your skin and sucked at the blood, like leeches. It was very painful!

My interest in religion led me to a meeting with one of the girls associated with the appearances of Our Lady of Kibeho. The Virgin Mary appeared several times between 1981 and 1989, introducing herself as 'Nyina wa Jambo' – Mother of the Word. Her appearances to Alphonsine Mumureke, Nathalie Mukamazimpaka and Marie Claire Mukangango were declared valid by the Roman Catholic Church. On one occasion she showed images of rivers of blood, deaths and unburied bodies, predicting the Genocide. Kibeho, which continues to be a revered pilgrimage destination, was sadly the site of some terrible massacres in 1994. Tutsis congregated there for protection, only to fall victim to the machete.

My meeting was with Salima Vestina, a Moslem, who also had visions of the Virgin Mary, but was not named by the Catholic Church. A friend of Drocelle's called Speciose was staying with us while she did a secretarial course in Kigali. She knew the visionaries and arranged for me to meet Salima with her in Butare. Salima really liked my name. Illuminée Nganemariya is quite unusual. Rwandans do not have a first name and family surname. Catholic families give their children a French name and a Kinyarwanda name. My Kinyarwanda name – Nganemariya – means 'follower of the Virgin Mary' and Illuminée means 'giver of light'. Mum and Dad dedicated their youngest child to the Virgin Mary.

Salima asked me what I wanted from the Virgin Mary, but I was very shy and stood there for five minutes without saying anything. I wanted to ask for help with my high school education, but the words just would not come out. Eventually Salima ended the embarrassing silence by saying that I would get what I deserved. She gave me a picture of the Virgin Mary and some money. I used the money to buy a picture of Jesus.

That night I had a very vivid dream. In it I was given a lift by two young men to a church, where people dressed in white were singing. The young men disappeared. But the people in the church told me to go away, this place was not for me. I saw a young boy tending sheep outside the church and asked him the way home. He told me that I had to follow the river. The river was very wide and deep, and I saw lots of people fall in and drown. I was very frightened, but then I heard a voice saying 'Do not worry, you are with me'. So we passed through the river and I ended up on a mountain, which I recognised as Mount Kigali. The voice said 'I love you very much', and I was handed to two soldiers who took me home.

I have thought about this dream a lot since the Genocide and am convinced that the Virgin Mary was showing me that I would survive. John, one of the young men in the car, took me with him following his death, but as he passed on he dropped me off, and I was told it was not my time. The river was the journey through the Genocide until I met the RPF soldiers on Mount Kigali and safety.

Chapter five

Eustache and Hutu Power

Radio Télévision Libre des Mille Collines (RTLM) was a Rwandan radio station which broadcast from 8 July 1993 to 31 July 1994, and played a significant role in the Genocide. Unlike the state radio station it played contemporary music, and quickly developed an audience among young Rwandans – who later made up the bulk of the Interahamwe militia. But alongside the sophisticated use of humour and popular tunes, it broadcast hate propaganda against Tutsis, moderate Hutus, Belgians, and the United Nations mission UNAMIR.

During the early 1990s the 'Hutu Power' extremists established Radio Mille Collines, which broadcast a continuous diet of anti-Tutsi propaganda. We used to listen to the propaganda and even managed to laugh at their threats.

But when the RPF invaded in October 1990, life became much more dangerous for Tutsis. The RPF was formed by Tutsi exiles, all officers and NCOs in the Ugandan army. Their initial attack was repulsed by President Habyarimana's soldiers helped by the French. The RPF leader Major-General Fred Rwigyema was killed. He was succeeded by Major Paul Kagame, who was forced to run a guerrilla war from the mountains of north west Rwanda.

The MRNDD, the main Government party and the CDR, who were Hutu extremists, dominated our village. Whenever the CDR had a meeting we had to stay indoors. At the end of the meeting the party members would drink very heavily and, if a Tutsi happened to be out and about, the CDR would stop their car and kill the occupants. They were never charged with murder. We were expendable. The radio would blandly state that such and such a person had been killed and that would be the end of the matter. This was alcohol-fuelled group violence, because Hutu extremists on their own were not a threat.

The Hutu extremists started to pick on my brother in early January 1992. He had married Odile Mukamudenge on December 28, 1991 and was at home enjoying his honeymoon. In Rwanda 'honeymooners' just take time off work and stay at home together rather than go on holiday. Eustache was working for the Red Cross and was a leading figure in the drive to bring electricity to our village. It was probably jealousy that sparked an outburst of Hutu anger. Several letters threatening to kill him were put under his door.

The honeymoon period was at an end and Odile had gone back to work, but Eustache was having an extra day off. A Hutu group came to the house and smashed their way through the front gate into the compound. Fortunately Eustache was alerted to the intrusion by his housekeeper, and managed to escape over the back wall. He fled to Kigali city centre, where he and Odile lived in a one-room flat provided by a Hutu friend.

They decided to live there until things calmed down in the village and were still in the flat at the start of the Genocide. Sadly, Eustache's housekeeper, who stayed behind to look after the house, was one of the first people to be killed by the local Interahamwe militia. He was Hutu, but they murdered him out of spite. Eustache was high on their list.

Chapter six

Mum – I am pregnant !

In August 1993, after several months of negotiation, the Arusha peace accord was signed between President Habyarimana's govermnent and the RPF. The peace accord allowed for the RPF to join a new power-sharing administration, but it did little to stop the continued unrest within Rwanda. Meanwhile, the Interahamwe (Kinyarwanda meaning 'those who work together' or 'those who fight together'), the Hutu civilian militia allegedly trained by the Rwandan military and French advisors, was becoming active.

I made a new friend at Ajesco College called Cecile. We became very close, and I used to sit with her in class. We were good for each other; Cecile's outgoing personality complemented my shyness. We soon got to know each other's families. She lived in Kigali with her aunt, as her parents lived in Butare to the south. Sadly, Ajesco College closed after my first year there. Cecile went to a government school and I went back to Apacope College. But although we were separated, we kept in touch.

Soon after she had started at the government school I met Cecile in a taxi. She told me with great excitement that she had a really nice new boyfriend called John Nsengiyumva. But unfortunately there was a problem, because her family would not accept him. He was Tutsi and she was mixed Hutu/Tutsi.

The next time I saw Cecile she was heavily pregnant. She had decided to ignore her parents' misgivings and had gone to live with John. She wanted me to meet him, but we never managed to arrange this: it was a Friday when I met her and, tragically, the following Monday she died giving birth to her son, David.

John was a friend of the Director of my college. They both came from

Kibuye in western Rwanda. On the day Cecile died, I went into college as usual. But it was announced that there would be no classes that afternoon because of Cecile's death. Her funeral was so sad. Cecile had been like a sister to me, and after she died I wondered what I could do for her child. I called on John's Aunt Azera and her family, as she was looking after David. This was how John started to get to know me.

John was the oldest of five children. His mum had died when he was young from liver problems, so he came to live in Kigali with Aunt Azera. John went to a mechanics' school and did very well in his course. He managed to get a job as a driver from someone in the Government, who helped him set up his own business as a driving instructor, based in the city centre. As well as giving driving lessons, he bought and refurbished cars and sold them on.

He began asking me personal questions. But I never thought I would become his wife, mainly because there were too many problems in Rwanda at the time. Anyway, as I have already explained, I was not very worldly wise and did not really know how to handle a relationship. Then one day John asked me. 'Do you have a friend?' So I said, 'What do you mean by a friend?' He replied. 'Do you have a man friend?' No, was the answer. But I do not think he believed me, because I had been to Apacope College where all the girls were very sharp!

I still did not think anything would happen. But my family's reaction to John pushed us closer together. I always wanted to be honest with them, so I told them that John and I were getting friendly. Mum and Dad were happy for us to be friends, but some of my family said that they did not want me to get involved with him. I was young and clever: I should finish my education and make a career, rather than get married and, no doubt, have children.

John suggested that he should get to know my family before anything else happened between us. But one thing quickly led to another, and I fell pregnant almost immediately. It was so ironic. I had been a good Catholic girl and now, in my early twenties, disaster struck as I was finally touched by a man. At first I thought I had malaria, but as the days and then weeks passed and I missed my period for a second time, I became more and more terrified of the consequences of being pregnant. How would I face my family? I could not contemplate going to our doctor, so John arranged for us to see a doctor that he knew, some distance from home – who confirmed my worst fears.

To be unmarried and pregnant was not good news in Rwandan society. In the old days pregnant girls were abandoned in the forest. I was at least spared that fate, but I dreaded telling my family. I even considered an abortion. When I finally plucked up the courage to go home, there was little comfort to be found, just anger and confusion. Eustache was very angry and would not talk to me. But Mum was understanding, she knew that I had not slept around.

My mother had wanted a proper church wedding for her youngest daughter. But that was out of the question. Fortunately we had always had a relationship where we could talk openly. Mum believed in her children making their own way. 'I gave birth to you, the rest is your responsibility. Good luck,' was her response. I decided that the best thing to do under the circumstances was to go and live with John. It did not seem right to stay at home, with all the neighbours' tongues wagging as my stomach expanded.

John was willing to go ahead with a proper wedding straight away, but my family would not accept this, so we decided to give them time to get used to my pregnancy. All the same, he took me to Nyarutaram to propose properly. It was a lovely area of countryside where lots of Rwandans went to propose marriage. The area has changed a lot since the Genocide, and has now been converted into a golf course.

By now it was the autumn of 1993 and tensions between Hutu and Tutsi were growing. A lot of people died or disappeared as a result of violence. The Interahamwe militia was everywhere checking ID cards and giving Tutsis a hard time. There were murmurings in the local community that something terrible was about to happen. One night before I moved in with John, he gave me a lift home. We had a Hutu friend of John's with us. He was in the army and in full uniform. Near our house the Interahamwe stopped the car and demanded that John hand his keys to them. They were very surprised when they saw a Hutu soldier in the car. Just as John drove off, one of the Interahamwe smashed his fist across my face. What had I done to him?

John was not worried about the growth of the 'Hutu Power' movement. Probably because he was young, he thought that everything would be fine, and that even if there was a fight between Hutu and Tutsi it would not last long. He had many Hutu friends and taught lots of Hutus to drive. He believed nothing really terrible could happen. I even suggested that we leave Rwanda, but he said 'No way'. Even in the Genocide he never gave up. He always said 'Do not worry, do not worry, everything will be all right.' John was a very positive person. He did not think he would die.

We went out a lot at the weekend. I really enjoyed his company. John was a very relaxed person and made me very happy. We would often go to a local restaurant where he would buy me my favourite meal, chicken grill with hot chillies, green bananas and salad.

John's family were lovely, especially Azera. We sometimes went to their Seventh Day Adventist church on Saturdays. But John was not a very strict churchgoer, and quite often used to work on Saturday. Aunt Azera would get angry with him, as this was strictly against the rules of his church. John often said that he would like to become a Catholic, because they could do what they wanted!

Communication with my family was difficult. However John did manage to get a relationship going with Mum, although she was still not happy for us to set a date for the wedding. Eustache would not come and see me. Admittedly he was angry with me, but it was also not the done thing in Rwanda for your family to visit when you were living with your partner and not married. Berencille and Calnie did come and visit me, but I would have been much happier if I could have welcomed everyone together. Then, in November 1993, Dad died.

Chapter seven

Marriage

Fortunately I managed to see Dad before he died. His death was heartbreaking. I was so sad that he would not be at my wedding. Mum finally agreed to the marriage, and at the beginning of January, John began planning our big day. He put a lot of energy into the preparations, wanting to show my family that he was very serious about our future together. He also found us a smart new home in the Nyakabanda district of Kigali. In Rwanda weddings are big celebrations, and everything has to be 'just right'. John's commitment to the wedding plan impressed my family and helped reconcile our differences.

Of course, what I did not know was that my time with John was going to be very brief. He was the sort of person who would never ever let you down. I feel really sad when I think about him, because he worked hard and deserved success. He should not have had his life taken away at such a young age.

I did less and less at home as my pregnancy developed. We had a young girl called Clementine who cooked and cleaned, and John even employed a young boy to iron our clothes and wash the car. I cooked when I felt like it, and only did the chores that I chose to do, like looking after our bedroom and the living room. It was a wonderful pampered existence. John was determined that I would be relaxed and give birth to a happy child. I had the normal strange food desires during the pregnancy and became a big fan of Guinness and coke – quite unusual for a non-drinker, and a very peculiar mixture!

We were married at Kaciyuru registry office on April 3, 1994. Our wedding was a wonderful occasion. My brother and I were finally reunited. I was very happy and wore a white dress even though I was eight months pregnant. John looked so handsome in his black suit. At last, I thought, all the people I loved were together and happy under one roof. My family and John's family were together for the first time. Lots of John's friends, both Hutu and Tutsi, joined us and drank to our future happiness.

We could put the stress of my pregnancy behind us and look forward to the birth of our child. We had already thought of names, Agathe for a girl and Roger for a boy. John said that he was very happy with his new mum and wife. He had given so much to our relationship. All I could give him was love.

Chapter eight

April 4 and 5

I lay sleepily in bed, as dawn rose on the first morning of our honeymoon. It was a day to treasure. I could already hear John going through his morning routine. But today would be different: for the first time since I had moved in, he had cancelled all work appointments and we were able to enjoy a few blissful hours on our own.

My first happy duty of the day was to tackle the wedding gifts that lay unopened around our bedroom. This was my first experience of presents; as I have already explained, a Rwandan's wedding is traditionally the only time that gifts are received. It was great fun exploring the pile of presents, trying to guess what was hidden behind the wrapping paper and deciding which one to open first. Of course I had received gifts before, mainly from Eustache on his various returns home, but I had never in all my 25 years had such a 'mountain' to investigate.

Naturally my first selection was a present from my big brother. John had joined me and watched as I removed the wrapping to reveal a traditional Rwandan wall hanging embroidered with words 'Urugo Ruhire', which roughly translates as 'wishing you the best in your new house.' After the misery of the previous eight months, we had every reason to believe that this wish would come true.

Next I opened Drocelle's gift, a set of table mats and matching seat covers. This was followed by the offering from Esperance, my close friend from childhood, who had been a great source of comfort and support during my pregnancy. Esperance had also given us matching table mats and seat covers! 'Oh well, we can keep one set for Sundays,' I joked. Having opened my top three gifts, I decided to delay the pleasure of discovering the delights of the remainder. I never did get to open them.

John sat in thoughtful silence as I set about the presents. When I had finished, he said 'Why did you open your brother's present first?'

'Because he is my brother', I replied.

'You love him very much, don't you?'

'Of course I do.'

Then John surprised me by saying, 'More than me?'

'You cannot ask me a question like that,' I said lightly. 'My feelings for my brother are completely different to the feelings I have for you.'

'No, I am sure you do love him more than me,' was his response.

To my amusement I realised that my new husband was feeling a little jealous and insecure. John and Eustache had only met on a handful of occasions before the wedding, usually in circumstances that were sad or stressful like my father's funeral.

They had kept apart during the thaw in relations with the family in the lead-up to the wedding, mainly owing to Eustache's refusal to speak to John unless absolutely necessary. Even so, I never left John in any doubt about my affection and respect for my brother.

John's dad, Murindahabi, came round to our house during the afternoon. He worked as an auxiliary in a hospital and had remarried after John's mum's death. Murindahabi had travelled up from Kibuye for the wedding. His visit was great fun. I laughed as he told stories from John's childhood. He said that John was the sort of child who would never sit in one place for long and was always playing with things like watches, taking them apart to see how they worked. He had loved all things mechanical, and was one of the youngest people in Kibuye to learn to drive. Murindahabi and I became firm friends, and we promised to visit him soon in Kibuye.

The next morning was ours do as we pleased. We made love, and for the first time I enjoyed it. Any desire for a physical relationship with John had disappeared the minute I found out that I was pregnant. The doctor told me that this was normal, but I think it was psychological. My feelings for John, at the time, were mixed. I appreciated his enthusiasm and energy as he set about building a life for us, but I also felt angry about what had happened – angry with myself as much as with him. I had been swept along by John's charm and appetite for life. I had allowed things to happen too quickly.

But what had happened, had happened. John did not force me to live with him; as in most cases, the decision was mine. After thinking through my options very carefully, I realised that a lot of men in John's position would have refused to accept that the child was theirs, or would have found other ways of avoiding the reality of the situation. John had the strength and independence of someone that had left home young and was not afraid of hard work. He was not daunted by the responsibility of setting up a comfortable family home.

Paradoxically, my only complaint was that we never had time to relax together. John was always busy working and providing for our new home, and was often too tired to make conversation. That was why the mornings of April 4 and 5 was so unique. I cannot remember another time when we were so at ease with each other.

Chapter nine

April 6

On the evening of April 6 1994 a plane carrying Rwandan president Juvenal Habyarimana, together with the president of Burundi, was shot down over Kigali airport.

Exactly who killed the president has never been established, but whoever was behind the rocket attack, its effect was both instantaneous and catastrophic. In Kigali, the presidential guard, elements of the Rwandan armed forces (FAR) and extremist militia (Interahamwe and Impuzamugambi) immediately initiated a campaign of retribution. Leaders of the political opposition were murdered, and the slaughter of Tutsis and moderate Hutus began.

On April 6, John and I had our first 'public engagement' as man and wife. We went round to my cousin Esther's house for dinner. She and her husband, Innocent Seminega, had a big, happy household; just the type of family home that I hoped that we would have in time. Not only did their three children, Anna, Amelia and Babish live with them, but there was also Innocent's brother and two sisters, a family friend called Donata, the resident childminder, Marie Bonne, and a cook, Claver.

Innocent was a lovely man. Kind, intelligent and handsome, he was the person who had diverted me from my plans to become a nun and put the thought of marriage into my head. Innocent told me that there was nothing better than the feeling of being in love. 'You are a pretty girl,' he said. 'One day you will meet someone kind.' I have a picture of him in my heart to this day.

On the way home we spotted large groups of Interahamwe militia assembling in public places. We thought nothing of this. Since the RPF's invasion in 1990, there had been increasing violence against Tutsis. Random attacks would take place in response to alleged RPF activity, and there were regular MRNDD and CDR demonstrations in Kigali city centre, which ended with Tutsi killings.

The government radio station would casually announce the latest crops of deaths – and of course nobody was ever brought to justice. This had been going on since 1959, but nothing prepared me for the planned destruction of the Tutsis that began on the night of April 6. Thankfully the Interahamwe did not stop us during the drive home. We were soon back in our bedroom, and clambered into bed, tired but very happy.

Chapter ten

April 7

Within 24 hours of Habyarimana's jet being shot down, roadblocks manned by the Interahamwe militia sprang up around Kigali. Tutsis were separated from Hutus and hacked to death with machetes at the roadside. Many taller Hutus were presumed to be Tutsis and were also killed. The militias were organised to work round the clock in shifts.

We were woken at 5am the following day by the sound of distant gunfire. John switched on the government radio station to listen to the news. The elation of the previous evening was soon replaced by a terrible foreboding.

The radio station was solemnly broadcasting details of the death of the Rwandan President Juvenal Habyarimana and the President of Burundi, Cyprien Ntaryamira. They had been killed when Habyarimana's private jet had crashed as it was about to land in Kigali, at 8.30pm on the evening of April 6. The blame for the crash was being placed squarely on the shoulders of the RPF, who had allegedly fired missiles at the plane.

The death of the president would no doubt result in very heavy anti-Tutsi reprisals. No wonder the Interahamwe had been out in force the previous night. I became convinced that we were going to die. What remained to be answered was how, where and when. My thoughts turned to my unborn baby, and I prayed for him or her to be born and not die inside me.

John took the opposite view to me. He thought there would be the usual day of fighting, then life would get back to normal. John's positive outlook was based on the knowledge that he had many Hutu friends. He gave them lifts, took their wives to hospital, taught them to drive and swapped salt, sugar and water with them. He felt that there was every reason to believe that these friendships would protect us.

So while I was preoccupied with how we were going to die, John's practical nature was focused on ensuring that we had enough food to eat. Concerned that we would run out of supplies, he went out to stock up on food. He returned, visibly shaken by what he had seen. Large groups of Tutsis were on the move, heading for Ikigo Iwacu Kabusunzu, an agricultural research station. They were planning to barricade themselves in the building, opting for strength in numbers rather than being picked off by the Interahamwe at home.

Early that afternoon, the Genocide claimed its first victims in our neighbourhood: Pastor Amoni and his family. Amoni was pastor of the local Seventh Day Adventist Church, and was well known to John's family. At around 2pm we saw a group of Interahamwe and soldiers, armed with guns and grenades, rushing past. Moments later a huge explosion rocked our house. Pastor Amoni's house was destroyed, and he and his family were killed in the blast.

Shortly after this incident, we witnessed what was to become a common sight. Hutu neighbours headed for the pastor's fields. Instead of mourning the family's death, they were stealing their beans and sweet potatoes. We later learned that the reason Amoni was top of the death list was because two of his sons had left four years earlier to join the RPF.

Obed, a distant relative of John's, visited about an hour after this incident. He was from a mixed Hutu/Tutsi family and wrote for one of the more independent Rwandan newspapers. He told us that the RPF had invaded from Uganda, and were fighting the Rwandan Army (FAR, Forces Armée Rwandaise). This news confirmed for me that the Interahamwe would target us. I pleaded with John for us to leave the house and join the other Tutsis at Ikigo Iwacu Kabusunzu. But John insisted that we stay put for the time being – at least until the situation became more clear.

Chapter eleven

April 8

The day after Habyarimana's death, the RPF renewed their assault on government forces, and numerous attempts by the UN to negotiate a ceasefire came to nothing.

On the ground at least, the Rwandans were largely left alone by the international community. Many nations evacuated their nationals from Kigali and closed their embassies as the violence escalated. Belgium withdrew from the multi-national UN peacekeeping force after the torture and murder of 10 of their soldiers. They were guarding the prime minister, Agathe Uwilingiyimana, a moderate Hutu.

During the morning the Interahamwe set up a roadblock outside our house and another two houses further on. From what we could see the Interahamwe did not know what to do at this stage. They had probably just been pressed into service, and were unsure of their job. What we did not appreciate, as we watched the activity, was that their orders were to inspect the ID cards of everyone who passed by. Anyone with a Tutsi ID card was to be killed.

Thousands of Tutsis were apprehended at roadblocks like the one outside our house. Some were in a position to bribe their way through; others managed to call on family connections and were given safe passage. Then there were those who met soldiers or Interahamwe who had no stomach for their task, or were sickened by the killing and let them carry on unharmed – until the next roadblock. But for the majority, the journey ended at their first roadblock. For a few Rwandan francs, Tutsis could pay to be shot by a soldier. The alternative was to be handed over to the brutal Interahamwe, who were fuelled by a dangerous cocktail of alcohol and drugs.

Many of their victims were stripped and subjected to appalling torture. Using machetes, the Interahamwe chopped off their arms and legs and gouged out their eyes, before dealing the killer blow. Or they would be attacked with spiked clubs, before being hurled into open mass graves and stoned to death. Some were just thrown into rivers with their hands and feet tied. Women were raped and murdered, or were kept for a while as sexual slaves and subjected to sickening abuse until their captors tired of them. Pregnant women suffered the worst fate. Their stomachs were ripped open, and their unborn child would be dangled before their eyes as they died in agony.

No place was safe or sacred. In 1959 people had huddled in churches for sanctuary. They did so again in 1994, but to no avail, as the Interahamwe slaughtered people as they cowered under pews.

As the scene for the Genocide was being set outside our house, John and I could already count ourselves lucky to be alive. The Tutsis sheltering at Ikigo Iwacu Kabusunzu were murdered during the early evening. If John had given in to my pleading, we would have died with them.

Chapter twelve

April 9

Soldiers and police officers encouraged ordinary citizens to take part in the Genocide. In some cases, Hutu civilians were forced to murder their Tutsi neighbours by military personnel. Participants were often given incentives, such as money or food, and some were told they could appropriate the land of the Tutsis they killed.

The next morning, Mama Koko, one of my Hutu neighbours, visited our house. Although I was fairly new to the area, I knew Mama Koko quite well. She would often call round and her little boy used to wash John's car. But now our world had changed and here she was, boldly asking for all my possessions – clothes, crockery – anything she could easily carry. She, of course, promised to 'protect' everything.

Mama Koko's family was very poor. I did not think this was an offer of help! She had already told me that she had taken green beans from the Pastor's fields. I was very frightened and, as a result, my possessions did not seem to matter any more. However, I decided to thank her for the offer and explained that I would like to keep my things for the time being.

During the day the Interahamwe started to get to work at the roadblock outside our house. People were screaming for their lives as they were savagely cut down. John and I decided that it was too dangerous to hide together, so we agreed to part. I went round to Mama Koko's and asked if she would hide me. She agreed, but would not allow me inside her house and sent me to her toilet, which was a simple hole in the ground covered by a rickety shed.

There was nowhere to sit, and the smell was disgusting. I managed to last three hours, but was very worried about the impact on my unborn child. My discomfort was made worse by Mama Koko who popped down to see me several times, worried that her 'generosity' would result in reprisals. She told me that I would have to go at the end of the day, because her husband was a member of the local Interahamwe.

When I returned home, I discovered that the Interahamwe had been to the house looking for John. But Clementine, our house girl, said that she did not know where he was. They did not harm her, but a Hutu friend of John's called Poku was not so lucky. He was also asked about John's whereabouts. When he said nothing, he was cut down with machetes and died in the street.

I was terrified, expecting the Interahamwe to return at any moment. Fortunately John appeared with a young Hutu friend called Rwemarika, who was a policeman. Rwemarika's mother was a Tutsi, and he offered us a room at her house nearby. But John decided it would be safer to go to his Aunt Azera's. So, under the cover of darkness, we headed for Azera's. It was just 10 minutes away on foot.

Azera's husband was mixed Hutu/Tutsi, so this afforded us some protection.

As well as three of their children, there was a cousin from Burundi in the house, who had sadly chosen the wrong time to make a family visit, along with two other Tutsis who were hiding from the Interahamwe. Azera's eldest daughter, Mukeshimana, was away staying with a relative in Gitarama.

We were at Azera's for a week. The tension was almost unbearable as we waited for the Interahamwe to catch up with us. When the inevitable happened and they came knocking, John was in a position to negotiate. He bought himself some time by handing over his car. The Interahamwe left us alone, but we knew that they would be back. Even John was beginning to worry.

Chapter thirteen

April 16

At UN headquarters in New York, the killings were initially categorized as a breakdown in the ceasefire between the RPF and FAR. Throughout the massacre, both the UN and the US refrained from labelling the killings as Genocide, which would have made emergency intervention necessary.

On April 16, the Government radio station encouraged Tutsis in hiding to return home. We were assured that the RPF was the enemy – the civilian population would be safe. So we dutifully headed back home, not really believing that this marked the end of the killing. I am sure that our departure must have been a relief for Azera, as her supplies were getting very low.

Of course this was just a ploy to smoke Tutsis out into the open, and the killings continued unabated. Like most people we sat and listened to the radio. There was nothing else to do. During the initial period following Habyarimana's death, the Government radio station broadcast a diet of mournful music and news. But now the tone had changed. Both the Government station and Radio Mille Collines were openly urging Hutu men to rape, kill and torture Tutsis. 'Come on guys', the presenters would say. 'What are you waiting for? Think of those Tutsi women in their short skirts and long legs. What about those handsome Tutsi men? Their time is over.'

One of our Tutsi neghbours, Theogen, with his wife Jeanne and baby son Renée, also came out of hiding. Theogen was soon caught by the Interahamwe. Jeanne and Renée survived, but both were to die of Aids. Sadly Theogen had infected his wife, and she passed HIV to her baby son.

We sat at home for two weeks, listening to the radio and waiting to die.

Outside the mayhem continued. Bodies were piling up in the street. Dogs were howling and fighting over the bodies. The smell was abominable. The noise was terrifying.

I could not eat any more. My legs began to swell. I became more and more worried about the safety of my unborn child. I prayed that when the Interahamwe finally came, it would be a quick death, but only after my baby had been born.

Chapter fourteen

April 30 and May 1

Many Tutsis took refuge in churches and mission compounds. These places became the scenes of some of the worst massacres. Hospitals also became prime targets as wounded survivors were sought out, then killed. Aid agencies were helpless; having let people injured or in flight into a compound or hospital, they were forced to leave them there – and few survived.

On April 21, the Red Cross estimated that hundreds of thousands of Tutsis and moderate Hutus – perhaps a quarter of a million – had already been slaughtered in the two weeks since the Genocide began. Together with the mass murder of Soviet prisoners of war during World War II, it was the most concentrated act of Genocide in human history.

My labour pains began on the morning of Saturday, April 30. Normally I would have been taken to hospital, but of course this was now out of the question. If I had tried to get to a hospital I would have been killed on the way. We also heard tales of patients being slaughtered in their beds, and babies being killed at the moment of birth.

When a baby is born in Rwanda, your family rallies round to help. But I could not contact my mum and sisters. In fact I had no idea whether they were still alive. I was terribly lonely, but was determined to stay alive until my baby was born.

Both Clementine and John were anxious that any noise would bring the Interahamwe. So John decided to go to Azera's to ask for help. She came to our house straight away, and told me to keep as quiet as possible. But it was very difficult; I was in terrible pain. Azera was a hairdresser – hardly the skills

I needed at this juncture in my life! But she was kind and understanding, and gave me the support that I needed. It was agreed that it would be too dangerous for me to give birth at our house, so John and I headed back to Azera's house through the banana plantations, dodging the Interahamwe. Every step was agony.

Azera and an older neighbour acted as my midwives. I did not care about keeping quiet. The pain was excruciating and I just had to yell out. They got me to walk round the house. It was absolutely exhausting, and very stressful. John came and went during the evening, worried that we would be killed together. Then, after 20 hours in labour, our son was finally born at 5am on May 1. I had achieved my objective. The Interahamwe could strike, and with luck my baby might survive.

He was a quiet and placid baby, who took to my breast very quickly – quite amazing considering the traumatic circumstances of his birth. I should have been enjoying the moment, resting and feeding him. Instead, just three hours after our son was born, John and I made the risky journey back through the banana plantation to our home.

I had a constant pain in my stomach and was bleeding quite badly. John was very worried and, despite the danger, went out at 11am to try and find some paracetamol. By now most Tutsi doctors had been killed, and the Interahamwe were stalking hospital corridors, so he had a very difficult errand to run.

John had been gone for an hour. I drifted in and out of sleep. Suddenly the peace was shattered by the sound of gunfire, as a group of 10 soldiers and Interahamwe burst into the house. Some of them seemed to be very high on alcohol or drugs. Once inside they rounded on Clementine, who was mixed Hutu/Tutsi. 'What are you doing in a Tutsi house?' they shouted. She was roughly taken to another room and was gang raped. The screams were terrible.

While this was happening, their leader addressed me with exaggerated courtesy. 'Look Madame, we are not here to kill you. We are sure that there are some good Tutsis, just as there are bad Hutus, like the former Prime Minister, Agathe Uwilingiyimana.' Agathe Uwilingiyimana had been one of the first people murdered at the beginning of the Genocide along with 10 Belgian UN soldiers who had been protecting her.

'We want to find the people who killed President Habyarimana.' He then explained that he wanted to question John about possible links with the RPF, who of course were being blamed for the death of the president. Tutsis like John and my brother Eustache, who were good businessmen and made money, were often suspected of receiving cash from the RPF. Young businessmen, along with professionals like doctors, teachers and lawyers were at the top of 'death lists' drawn up by the Interahamwe. Community leaders were also targeted first, and top of the list was anyone suspected of 'links' with the RPF, just like Pastor Amoni.

The initial 'campaign' in the Genocide was well organised. Each community had its roll-call of prominent Tutsis. This was not a spontaneous outburst of anger, but a well-planned project which developed into hell on earth as the killing rate increased.

I am sure that John did not have any 'link' with the RPF. If he did, he kept it very secret. It is possible that he had friends who had joined the 'rebels' and – like most Tutsis – sympathised with what they were trying to achieve politically. Kagame and the RPF had embarked on a struggle to ensure that they had a place at Rwanda's 'top table' and, as a result, could undo years of oppression that had seen Tutsis become second-class citizens. But John also had Hutu friends in the FAR (Forces Armée Rwandaises). He would not have relished the task of being involved in an all-out civil war.

The Interahamwe leader was polite but persistent. 'Where is John? 'He has money, someone to help at home, a good standard of living.' 'How does he get his money?'

I told him that I did not know where John had gone – which was the truth. Then his drunken foot soldiers returned from raping Clementine.

One of them was both angry and impatient. 'Let us kill her,' he said. I was fully prepared for the machete blows that would follow. At least my son had been born. But to my surprise, the others did not respond to this lone voice. They wanted John, and had worked out that the best chance of finding him was by keeping his wife and baby son alive. He was bound to return home.

They hung around the house for about an hour. I was asked for money, but had none and offered them a Bible instead. This made them laugh and, ignoring my gift, they looked around the house for anything that could be

48

sold. They took my wedding ring and John's glasses. In better times I would have fought to keep the ring, but now I did not care about anything except John's safety.

Clementine was their other 'possession'. She was dragged off for further abuse at the hands of these animals.

Chapter fifteen

May 2 to May 9

In some local villages, the militias forced Hutus to kill their Tutsi neighbours or face a death sentence for themselves and their entire families. They also forced Tutsis to kill members of their own families.

John was just round the corner from home when he heard the gunshots. He thought that I had been killed, and went to Rwemarika's mum's house for help. She hid him in the pit they used for ripening green bananas for home brewed urwagwa. Every night for a week she visited him with food and water.

What he did not know was that she was also making nightly visits to me. I was in a terrible state, with no food and water. She gave me water with sugar. Normally I would not have accepted gifts from her, as she was very poor, but now I had no choice. I spent most of the time lying in bed, not having the energy to move. I was numb with fear, and had given up all hope. Every night I had to cope with the trauma of the Interahamwe charging into the house, to see if John was with me.

Rwemarika's mum told John that we were dead to prevent him from returning home and the inevitable confrontation with the Interahamwe. But on May 9, she relented and told him that we were alive, at the same time pleading with him not to go. 'I have to be with my wife and child,' was his brave response. 'It is selfish to remain here. I have to try to help. If we are to die, we must die together.' So, on the evening of May 9, he crept out of the banana pit and headed home.

It was around midnight when I heard someone at the door and thought it was the Interahamwe again. John emerged from the darkness. He looked dreadful. His eyes were red, and his clothes and shoes were covered in dirt from the banana pit. John's skin was normally very dark, but it had become strangely pale.

He asked me about the killers. I told him that he must hide as soon as possible, because they could return at any time. After a quick clean up and change of clothes, John fretted about where we could hide, and asked to hold the baby.

It was a Rwandan custom to give couples seven days before confirming the name of their new baby. We had already thought of Agathe for a girl in honour of the 'bad Hutu' Prime Minister, and Roger for a boy, named after Roger Bobo, a UN representative. The seven days were up, but we were in no mood to worry about names, so without further ado he was called Roger.

After holding Roger for 10 minutes, John decided to hide in our loft. He spent a miserable night, punctuated with sneezing fits. It was hopeless; the loft was probably one of the first places that the Interahamwe would search.

Chapter sixteen

May 10

Those behind the Genocide planned it to be carried out methodically, in cold blood. The Interahamwe were fuelled largely by a fanatical dedication to a political cause. Those who were high on drink, drugs or mindless violence had the potential to derail the Genocide programme. When these 'disorderly elements' began to join in and kill on whim, local administrators called for police assistance.

At about 9am John came down from the loft. Soon afterwards he called me to the window, as he had spotted a group of 20 men armed with machetes, axes and grenades heading for the house. I did not join him, as I knew who they were.

The Interahamwe burst into the house. They had found their man. Masumbuko was in charge. He was a member of Habyarimana's MRND party. Quite often the Interahamwe wore masks when they confronted their victims, but these men were not wearing masks and we could see their faces. What made the situation worse was that John knew them all, and counted some as his friends.

The interrogation began. 'Where have you been?' 'Do you get money from the RPF?'

John denied having any links with the RPF and explained that his money came from the driving school business.

I could sense the anger rising in the room. John, who was holding Roger, was told to hand the baby to me. Suddenly a nail stick was smashed into his face, and blood began pouring from his mouth. I am sure that, up until that moment, John thought that his friends and neighbours would not harm him.

One of the group was a man called Alphonse Gasasira, a coach driver who lived over the road from Azera. He had been a guest at our wedding just five weeks earlier. I remembered joking with him as he drank beer and chatted to our relatives. John turned to him. 'Why are you doing this to me?' 'You are my friend.' 'Remember the laughter at our wedding, remember the lifts that I gave to your family.' But it was to no avail. John was unable to break the spell that had changed friend and neighbour into an enemy.

There was a discussion about what they were going to do with us. Some of them wanted to take John to a roadblock and kill him. They also suggested that I should go with him. Masumbuko intervened, saying that they would take John but that I was to remain in the house. 'Whatever you have to say to your wife, say it now,' was the order. I knew then that it was all over.

They walked away leaving John, Roger and me standing at our front gate. We stood there for five minutes without uttering a word. John just looked at us. His face was expressionless, despite the pain from his bleeding mouth. I have no idea why he did not speak. Maybe he was still hoping that we would meet again, refusing to believe that his friends would kill him.

Masumbuko returned and seized John, and instinctively I followed. But one of the other men, ignoring the baby in my arms, violently pushed me backwards. 'Where are you going?' he asked. 'You Tutsis are all stupid. Your husband is going to the roadblock with all the other men. Go inside your home.'

Maybe he did me a favour – I would live. But in the days to come I often wished I had been allowed to share my husband's fate.

The Interahamwe shuffled off down the street. It was the last I saw of John. Not long afterwards I heard gunshots, and I knew that he was dead.

Chapter seventeen

May 10 – after John

Although the number of women killed in the Genocide was substantially lower than the number of murdered men, many women, along with girl children, were massacred. They were also exposed to a wide range of horrific abuses. Rape was extremely widespread, and thousands of women were individually raped, gang-raped, held in sexual slavery or sexually mutilated. These crimes were frequently part of a pattern in which Tutsi women were raped after they had witnessed the torture and killings of their relatives, and the destruction and looting of their homes. According to witnesses, many women were killed immediately after being raped.

Ten minutes after I had heard the gunshots, Mukamana, a girl who worked for Azera, ran into the house. She told me what had happened. In a final attempt to save his life, John had managed to persuade Masumbuko to take him to Azera's house. He obviously hoped to bribe him with money, but there were no Rwandan francs in the house. John offered to give them a cheque. What use was a cheque in this chaotic country? These drug and drink-crazed killers wanted hard cash. John's final gambit had failed, and the gang set about him with their machetes outside the house.

Alphonse Gasasira – his friend and our wedding guest – hacked off both his arms, before Masumbuko stepped forward to put John out of his agony with two shots to the head. His body was dragged away, no doubt to be dumped in one of the pits near a roadblock.

My immediate reaction to the news was to ask. 'Why did they not kill us as well? Why did they spare John's wife and son?' Because as far as I was concerned at the time, there was no life after John.

Mukamana went home. I was left on my own until 7pm when Pascale, one of the killers, returned. Pascale was nicknamed Muzungu, because of his pale skin. He had been a good friend of John's. He worked as a casual labourer and was a member of the CDR [Coalition for the Defence of the Republic, a bitterly anti-Tutsi party]. He carried a gun and seemed to take great pride in his new 'job' – murderer.

He walked into my bedroom. My first thought was that he was going to rape me, just as he had raped Clementine. This was my worst fear. I preferred death to rape. Pascale told me that John was dead and, to my surprise, asked if he could do anything to help me. Was this a guilty man, secretly mourning the death of his friend, trying to make amends?

I have often wondered why John survived for so long. As a prominent local Tutsi businessman, he would surely have been at the top of the Interahamwe's list. They must have had a lot of discussions about him. I suppose their consciences held them back until they finally 'did their work'. I told Pascale that there was nothing he could do. I wanted nothing from him.

Why didn't he rape me? Was this a manifestation of his guilt? He could not bring himself to touch his friend's wife. Maybe he was not interested because of the baby, although callous killers raped a lot of women in my condition. Once again I had been lucky. Pascale decided to let Clementine return and, despite the tragic circumstances, we had a happy reunion.

Chapter eighteen

May 11 to June 12

By mid-May, an estimated 500,000 Tutsis had been slaughtered. Confronted with international human rights and media reports depicting Genocide, the UN Security Council voted to send a force of 5,500 soldiers to Rwanda. However it failed to establish any timetable, and the troops did not arrive in Rwanda until months after the massacres ended.

During the morning of May 11, the Interahamwe returned and told me that I was to go to Azera's house for questioning. But instead they took me to a very small house nearby, where they asked me about the RPF. I knew nothing, and could not answer their questions.

Roger and I were kept in the house for four days. Azera sent her children over with food for me. I was so lonely – I wanted to die. Then, early on May 15, the Interahamwe told me that Azera and Festus and other people staying with them had been killed. I thought, 'Why not kill me now as well, and get it over with?' But this was not in their plan. I was ordered to go to Azera's house and look after their children: seven year old Aroni, Bernard, who was five, and their four year old sister Bettie, along with John's son David, who by now was two years old.

It transpired that the local Interahamwe boss, who had been a work colleague of Festus, had looked after the children while his men were murdering their parents and the cousin from Burundi. This was beyond my comprehension. But I should not have been surprised; morality had been consigned to the dustbin in the Rwanda of May 1994.

A girl called Uwimana, aged 20, had also survived. She was a cousin of Azera's and helped her look after the children. Uwimana had been raped as

Azera was killed, and now, each night, five killers wearing masks and carrying torches came for her. To this day I cannot bear the sight of torches. They took her at 1am and dropped her back at 9am, then Uwimana went straight to bed. This happened every night for two weeks. The children, who loved her, would jump on her bed and ask, 'Why are you crying?' 'Are you sick?' She was a big, strong girl, and throughout her ordeal she kept apologising for not feeling well enough to help look after the children.

Then it was my turn. He was a student, the son of a priest from Kibuye and knew John. I had been in the same class as his brother at high school.

I asked him to kill me – anything but rape. I did not want to be used. But he went ahead anyway. I was not angry. This was not a personal attack; all Tutsi women were being raped. But he was very rough. I have this awful memory of the gun and grenade dangling from his belt. When he had finished, he had the cheek to try and offer the hand of friendship. He wanted to help me get out of Rwanda, and asked if I had a passport. Just like Pascale, his morality was struggling to emerge from the darkness of his life as a member of the Interahamwe horde.

I felt disgusting and wanted to die. I confided in a Tutsi nurse called Esperance, who lived nearby and called to see me. 'Illuminée, if he comes again, say that you want to be with him. At least that will mean you will only have one man and not a group.'

Thankfully I had no need for her advice. The student rapist did not return. But I did pass her advice to poor Uwimana. What was happening to her every night was beyond my imagination. Up to 20 people, all wearing masks with slits for the eyes, would abuse her. Uwimana agreed to try Esperance's plan, but was worried how I would cope on my own. The plan succeeded. She did not return to the house, and later I heard that she survived the Genocide – only to die from Aids a few years later.

The spectre of Aids continues to hang over Rwanda. Tutsi women used as sex slaves who managed to survive, gave birth to Genocide orphans infected with HIV. This particular 'Hutu Power' legacy will cast a long shadow over Rwanda for many years to come.

We still had running water in Azera's house, but the electricity had been cut off. Esperance and another neighbour called Beatrice, both Genocide widows, brought scraps of food for us every day. Esperance's brother was hiding with her. He had come to stay just as the Genocide began, and was trapped in her house. But a brave young Hutu priest offered to take them to St Michael's Church, where Tutsis were heading for safety. On reflection, they decided that it was too dangerous for Esperance and her brother to make for the church, as he was too 'Tutsi-looking'. So Esperance suggested to the priest that he take me and the children instead.

I did not see any point in leaving the house. I did not have a forged Hutu ID card – essential for getting past the roadblocks – and Roger was a typical Tutsi baby. The priest agreed. He said that it would be too risky to take me, but offered to help Azera's three children escape. David would have to stay with me, as he was deemed to be too young to make the journey on foot.

Aroni, the oldest child, refused to leave his father's house. I tried to convince him.

'Please go. At any time they could return, burn the house down and kill us all. Go where you will be safe.'

Stubbornly he refused to leave. So only Bernard and Bettie followed the Hutu priest's plan. They left the house by themselves, each carrying a container. Their 'cover' was that they had been sent out to get water, a common activity for young children in Rwanda, as most houses did not have plumbing. The priest told them to follow a back route to avoid the first roadblock. He left, promising to meet up with them beyond the roadblock. The process was to be repeated until they skirted each roadblock and arrived at St Michael's, which was nearly three miles away.

Incredibly these little children aged four and five managed to follow all the priest's instructions. He faithfully met them after each roadblock and they duly turned up at the church. Their story has a happy ending, as they were taken into RPF controlled territory and a future in post-Genocide Rwanda.

About a week later, some FAR soldiers came with a message from a female cousin of John's who was living with a soldier. She had grown up in Burundi, where her family had fled during the 1959 Winds of Destruction. But she had moved back to Rwanda and had stayed with Azera for a while. She had been asked to leave due to her relaxed attitude to men and relationships. Marriage and divorce had followed (at the time almost unheard of in Rwanda), and now she was living with a FAR soldier.

The soldiers had been given instructions to collect Azera's children and take them to safety. I asked them to take David as well. They checked and were told that they were only authorised to remove Aroni from the house. This time Aroni agreed to go, leaving me alone in the house with Roger and David. We survived on more hand-outs from Beatrice and Esperance.

I was convinced that the Interahamwe would kill us soon. They visited every night, with masks covering their faces, to remove items from the house. Gradually all the furniture disappeared. The end would come when they had emptied the house.

Then, on the night of June 12, I overheard Pascale talking to his cronies outside. He said, 'We can put them in there' – meaning the pit for the new sewerage system that Azera and Festus had been installing. The man who had offered to help me following John's murder was casually planning our death. Minutes later he burst into the house brandishing a gun. He said that he was going to shoot us. I thought, 'Well at least it will be quick, I will not bleed to death in agony from machete blows.'

He cocked the pistol and fired. There was a click, but no bang. Pascale had run out of bullets.

He stormed out of the house. I was sure he would be back in minutes. But my next visitor was Clementine, who had pleaded with Pascale to leave us for the night.

Clementine had by now offered to become his 'wife' to end the gang rapes. So my last night alive would be spent in this dark and sad house. I sat there resigned to my fate, hoping that Pascale would return soon and finish his 'work'. But miraculously he did not come back. Instead I welcomed a friendly Hutu soldier called Rurangwa, who arrived at the house in tears.

Chapter nineteen

June 13

Rurangwa had been a good friend of John's. 'How could they do that to John after everything he did for them?' he cried. 'Oh lluminée, I would take you as my wife, but I respected John too much to do that. But you are in a bad condition. I loved John very much. What can I do for you?'

Rurangwa knew Esperance – they were both from Kibuye – and called on her. Later they both came to see me. Esperance said, 'Illuminée, please accept what we have planned for you. Rurangwa wants to take you to St Famille.' This is Kigali's Roman Catholic cathedral, and was a magnet for Tutsis during the Genocide. It also witnessed some of the worst examples of collusion between Hutu priests and the Interahamwe. Tutsis were 'selected' to be killed on a daily basis.

Wearily, I made my usual objections. 'I do not have an ID. They will not let me through the roadblocks.' But Rurangwa insisted. 'Illuminée, do everything I say and you will be safe.' I realised that I if I stayed in the house, Pascale or one of the others would eventually kill me, so it was worth trying to get to 'safety' at St Famille.

I definitely made the right decision. Soon after we left, the Interahamwe fanned through the neighbourhood mopping up any widows who were still alive, including Beatrice and Esperance.

Chapter twenty

June 14

The cathedral of St Famille is close to Kigali's commercial centre. Set in extensive grounds and surrounded by a high wall, it must have seemed the ideal sanctuary to people whose lives were at risk. Both Hutus and Tutsis fled there in droves when the violence began. As the weeks passed and the church became more crowded, many refugees were turned away. Of the Tutsis who did gain entrance, most had to pay a bribe at the gate. The priest in charge of the church, Father Wenceslas Munyeshyaka, divided the refugees according to ethnicity and discriminated against the Tutsis.

The first massacre at St Famille took place on 15 April, claiming the lives of more than 100 Tutsi men and boys. Fr Munyeshyaka witnessed the abductions, but although he had a phone, survivors said he made no effort to call for help.

We left at 5am. Rurangwa told me to tie Roger to my back, and he carried David. We walked to the nearest roadblock, where a driver and car were waiting for us. Rurangwa sat in the front beside the driver, and I took the back seat with the children. 'If we get stopped I will answer any questions about your identity,' said Rurangwa. 'If they ask you about your papers, just say that they have been lost.'

I knew that Rurangwa was taking a big risk for me. I was terribly nervous as we set off, hardly daring to look out of the car windows. My nerves began to settle as we were waved through several roadblocks: the military uniforms were our passport. But when we reached a major checkpoint in the city centre, Rurangwa was ordered out of the car. I kept my head down, praying that all would be well. After a five-minute interrogation, he returned. We were on our way again – what a relief!

By now it was 7am. Under normal circumstances, the journey would have taken 20 minutes. St Famille was in sight, and we pulled up at the final roadblock. Rurangwa began talking to the Interahamwe. My heart was pounding – we were so close.

'Everybody out', shouted one of the guards. This was it. I was terrified. We stood in a line, Rurangwa who was holding David, me with Roger on my back and the driver, who must have been regretting his kind offer to take this Tutsi woman to St Famille. It all depended on whether the Interahamwe believed our story, and if we looked like Tutsis. Every Rwandan carried around with them a mental image of a typical Hutu or Tutsi. The family history flashed before me. John's dad looked more Hutu than Tutsi; David's mum Cecille was a Hutu, as was his grand… My thoughts were interrupted.

One of the Interahamwe suddenly screamed, 'I cannot believe it!' He was looking straight at me. To my horror, I realised that I knew him. A few years older, a little sturdier perhaps – but unmistakably, this man, wearing the dark uniform of the infamous Interahamwe, had once been a fellow pupil at Apacope College.

Rurangwa was ordered to hand over his gun. 'I will not hand over my gun,' he protested. 'I am a soldier in the FAR.' My fellow pupil said, 'Well if you are a soldier in the FAR, what are you doing bringing cockroaches to the church? You are not doing your job.'

Realising that he was in a tight corner, Rurangwa replied. 'I do not know her. She gave me money to bring her here.' I did not blame Rurangwa; he was trying to save his life.

Then my old school 'friend' turned to me and said, 'Illuminée, how are you still alive?'

I do not think he expected an answer. 'I am very happy to see you,' he continued. 'But I am sorry, I cannot allow you to go to the cathedral.'

He looked at Roger and said to Rurangwa, 'Is this your child?'

'No'

'Is it Illuminée's?'

'Yes.'

'Then why doesn't she look like her?'

'It is not my problem', replied Rurangwa.

'She'. He thought Roger was a girl. This was lucky, because male babies were often killed on the spot, their bodies dashed against the nearest tree or wall. Rurangwa's gun was taken from him and he was led away. I was sure that he would be shot.

A car pulled up and my old school 'friend' suddenly became aggressive. He ordered me into the car, emphasising the command with a sharp jab in the back from his machete. I cannot say that I felt any pain, because my senses were numb. 'This is finally it,' I thought.

My former school colleague clambered into the car and we set off in the opposite direction, away from St Famille. Eventually he broke the silence, asking 'Are you Calnie's sister?' I had not seen or heard of my sister since the wedding, which now seemed a lifetime ago in a different world. 'Is she alive?' I asked. He said nothing.

The car arrived at a roadblock near my family home, manned by four men in FAR uniforms. A large pit was nearby. We were bundled out of the car. The former Apacope student barked at the soldiers 'Do your work', and drove off.

During the Genocide, 'Hutu Power' leaders referred to the murder of Tutsis as a duty for all Hutus. This was their 'work'. The radio stations continuously urged good Hutu men to do their 'work'. Many – like Pascale – enjoyed the responsibilities of this new employment. Others decided that this was a cruel task that had to be done, and became weary of their 'work'. However, failure to display sufficient enthusiasm for their 'work' could put them and their families in danger of being branded as Tutsi sympathisers.

We were in luck. The FAR soldiers at the roadblock belonged to the second group and seemed to have lost their appetite for 'work'. They seemed to like David, who was a lively little boy, and played with him for a few minutes. Then they decided to focus on me.

'Madame, why haven't they done their work? Why are you here?'

I had no answer to the first question, but told them that I had been heading for St Famille, and had been brought to them instead. One of the soldiers picked David up.

'I think this child needs something to eat.' He walked off holding David's hand.

I thought, 'That is the last time I will see him.'

'Where is your ID card?'

'I have lost it.'

They laughed. 'Madame, you do not have to carry your identity card. You are your identity.' He meant that one look at me was enough to convince anyone that I was a Tutsi. I was told to sit on a pile of bricks, a few yards from the pit. I was sure that there were bodies in the pit, but I was too frightened to look.

A few minutes later, David returned, munching on a sponge cake (like a doughnut). This was a good sign; perhaps we would live.

'I do not think this child is yours.'

'He is.'

'Where is your husband?'

'I do not know,' I said, remembering Rurangwa's instructions.

'You do not know! You do not know! Madame, you have lost your ID card. You have a baby, but you do not know where your husband is… I cannot believe you are here. I just cannot believe that they did not finish it.'

I was lucky. I was unfinished business. An uncalled-for task, passed on to someone else.

We waited for five hours with the sun burning down and no water to drink. As usual, Roger was quiet and seemed happy. I was always amazed at his calm nature and sometimes worried that he had been damaged by the trauma of his early days. During the morning, I saw several Hutus that I knew, who were 'bad news' for my family. But they passed by and said nothing.

The morning dragged on. Then at 1pm, my old school 'friend' returned and was astonished to see us sitting calmly in the sun. He screamed at the soldiers, 'I cannot believe that you have not done it. You take the person and you have to finish it. You have your work to do.'

I thought that this outburst would shame the soldiers into action and expected them to complete their 'work'. Instead I was ordered back into the car, and we headed off in the direction of St Famille. I thought that they were taking us to the cathedral, but we drove past and ended up at a large two-storey house.

I knew the area well from my student days. Most houses in Kigali were simple single-storey bungalows. A second storey was an indicator of wealth. We were in Nyarugenge, a district popular with wealthy Tutsi families and convenient for a private school for their children. Most of these people were probably dead by now. The abandoned houses had been looted and were used for interrogation, torture and killing.

We entered the house and were taken to a small room with clothes and other possessions scattered on the floor. There were blood stains on the walls and floor. The room smelt of death. I asked one of the Interahamwe guards, 'Who is going to kill us?' But he did not answer. He locked the door and left me, Roger and David alone in that dreadful room.

The children were very quiet. Perhaps they instinctively knew that it would be safer that way. I felt extremely tired and tried to coax them into sleeping. I used my feet to clear a space between the clothes and excrement that covered the floor and, even though both children must have been very hungry and thirsty, we settled down to sleep.

Our rest abruptly ended in the early evening, when four young men burst into the room. They ordered us to leave. Once again I asked if we were going to be killed – but there was no reply.

We were bundled into a car. The driver looked at me as if he was searching his memory. I did not recognise him, but after my meeting with the old school 'friend' at St Famille I was prepared for another uncomfortable reunion. The moment passed and, after a 10-minute drive, we stopped outside another house.

We were taken inside and there, to my surprise and delight, was Rurangwa. I was very pleased to see him, as I thought that he had been killed at St Famille.

He glanced at me, but said nothing. Two other men were in the room: a tall light-skinned man in his mid 20s who was obviously the leader, and another man who remained silent during the questioning, but whose body language communicated total hostility.

The leader, who I later found out was called Bosco, pointed to Rurangwa and asked if I knew him. Rurangwa had denied knowing me at St Famille. But I decided it was time to tell the truth. I had nothing to lose.

'Yes,' I replied.

'How do you know him?'

'Rurangwa was a friend of my husband.'

'Did Rurangwa do anything to you?'

'No.'

'Did you give him any money?'

'No.'

'Do you mind if Rurangwa says something to you?'

'No.'

'Illuminée, I am sorry there is nothing else I can do for you,' was Rurangwa's contribution.

Suddenly the silent hostile man jumped up and stormed out of the room. Bosco and Rurangwa looked at each other and burst out laughing. Laughter was beyond me, so I did not join in. I think the other man was angry because I was still alive. Bosco and Rurangwa must have been laughing at his impatience.

Bosco regained his composure and said, 'You are a Tutsi. If we help you, what will you do for us?'

I remained silent. I did not have the energy to start bargaining for my life. Rurangwa broke the silence. 'I think Bosco wants to help you.'

I was not so sure.

The interrogation was over. I was led to another room where a Hutu girl offered me food and drink. I gratefully accepted the drink. But the day's events – it seemed a lifetime since we had set off with Rurangwa at 5am – and the stress of thinking that I was going to die at any moment, had destroyed my appetite.

'Give the food to him,' I said, pointing at David. He was soon tucking into potatoes and beans. I had been with the Hutu girl for about 10 minutes, when a new batch of Interahamwe entered the house. They ignored me. But when the girl offered me somewhere to sleep, I nodded and was pleased to get away from the killers.

Bosco returned at 10pm. He was in a hurry and was carrying a gun. 'Put your child on your back and follow me.' Was he going to kill me? Wearily I obeyed. He picked up David and we left the house.

As we stepped into the darkness, Bosco whispered, 'Madame, the people in the house want to kill you, but I will look after you.'

'Why?' was my only response.

He did not answer, but just repeated that people were not happy about me being alive and that we had to move quickly.

We walked for about 20 minutes, using alleys to avoid being seen. Our route took us to the Kinamba district, an area that I knew very well. We stopped outside a small house. Bosco knocked on the door. It was opened by a Tutsi-looking girl, aged about 20.

'Odile, look after this woman. I cannot stay' – and with that Bosco disappeared in to the night.

Perhaps because Odile looked like a Tutsi, I launched into a flood of questions trying to clarify what was happening.

'Hold on, hold on,' she said. 'Stop panicking. Put the children to bed and then we can talk.' With David and Roger settled, we sat down for a chat.

'Do you know that man?' Odile was referring to Bosco.

'No. I do not understand why he is helping me.'

'Do not worry. He will not kill you.'

'But he has a gun.'

'Look, because Bosco brought you here, he will not kill you.'

As I calmed down, I asked her how she knew him. It transpired that they came from the same area, Gisozi, on the edge of Kigali.

'How did you get here?' I was keen to know how she had survived.

'It is a long story. There is no time to tell you tonight. You must go to bed now. My husband will be unhappy if he sees you, at least until Bosco has talked to him.'

I took her advice and headed to the small room where David and Roger were sleeping soundly. I could not sleep. I played over and over in my mind the events of the day. It seemed that I had been chosen to survive – but why?

Chapter twenty one

Bosco's problem

On June 16 the RPF launched a commando raid behind enemy lines to rescue refugees at another central Kigali church, St Paul's. Hundreds of people were rescued and taken behind RPF lines. The next day, between 70 and 100 Tutsi men and boys along with two women were slaughtered at St Famille cathedral in retaliation. Their bodies were left strewn all over the church courtyard.

Bosco returned at 5am. I did not see him, but heard him instruct Odile.

'Tell her to stay in the room. She cannot go out. The children must stay with her at all times.'

Odile came into my room and passed on the orders. The confinement was particularly difficult for David – but the door remained closed. Over the next couple of days, the noise of gunfire in the city increased. What I did not know was that the FAR were in a pitched battle for Kigali with the RPF.

By now, the international community had finally woken up to what was happening in my beautiful country. Harrowing accounts by foreign correspondents and TV footage of corpses finally made the world wake up to the humanitarian disaster that resulted in some 800,000 deaths.

Of course the wider picture was well beyond my comprehension in this small bedroom. But the 'Hutu Power' leaders realised that their time was running out and began to plan a mass evacuation of the country. This made those whom they had put to 'work', the Interahamwe, increasingly nervous about their future. They were even more dangerous, lashing out like a wounded lion.

Bosco returned during my third day of confinement. 'Madame, I have a problem. The people think you are dead, and the person who recognised you at St Famille keeps asking to see your body.'

I had begun to think more clearly and remembered that there was a convent in Kigali associated with Mother Theresa of Calcutta. They used to take in orphans. Perhaps Bosco could leave David and Roger there, if he had to hand me over to the Interahamwe.

'I understand your problem,' I said. 'If you have to tell them that I am still alive, please take the children to the Sisters.'

He said that he would try, and left the house mumbling about his 'problem'.

Odile came into my room and had clearly been given an update on my situation. 'I am sure that Bosco will not send you out to be killed. The only potential problem is that they might search the house.'

When would this nightmare end? At least Odile was kind, and I was glad to have another adult with me. She finally told me her 'long story'. Her 'husband', nicknamed Pine, was mixed Hutu/Tutsi. He had become involved with the Interahamwe so he could protect the Tutsi side of his family. As a member of the Interahamwe, he at least had some influence over who lived and who died.

This was a bizarre, mad and sad way to live. Men like Pine would spend all day killing Tutsis, before returning home to an evening meal prepared by their Tutsi wives or mothers. But that was Rwanda's particular brand of madness during the spring of 1994.

Odile was one of the Tutsi survivors who had opted for 'marriage' to a killer instead of life as a sex slave and eventual death. In return for protection, she was little more than a prostitute, keeping her 'husband' happy in bed, cooking his meals and cleaning his blood-stained clothes.

We did not see Bosco again for another two days. He arrived in the middle of the night and said that we all had to leave the house immediately, including Odile and Pine. Despite the early hour – it was around 2am – there were plenty of people out and about, shouting and moving around. Everyone seemed very restless. After a 15-minute walk we arrived at a large house, where a tall Hutu-looking man in his 50s greeted us. His problem temporarily solved, Bosco melted into the night.

Two families were sharing the house. One was Pine's family. They looked very Tutsi. I later discovered that they were one of the small number of Tutsis who had managed to change identity after The Winds of Destruction in 1959. With the help of corrupt or compliant government officials, their ID cards had been changed to Hutu. Some of these people were killed during the Genocide because of the way they looked, but at least having the 'magic' word Hutu in their ID card gave them a better chance of survival.

The man who had opened the door was very friendly. I was introduced to his three daughters. They were very concerned about me and wanted to know my whole story. They immediately fell in love with David and fussed over him. After this wonderful welcome, I was taken to a bedroom where I was introduced to a very frightened Tutsi-looking lady. I almost felt like laughing, but I could not bring myself to feel any joy at being inside what appeared to be a very safe house.

'How on earth did you get here?' she said.

'But what about you,' I replied. 'What are you doing here?'

She introduced herself as Patricie. Her husband was the big man who had opened the door. His name was Munyangabo. He was a Hutu and was in serious trouble for protecting his Tutsi wife. The Interahamwe had tried to take Patricie on several occasions. But each time Munyangabo had paid them off.

Patricie held Roger. She could not believe that I had given birth to this healthy child and had survived the death squads. It was a miracle. We talked, and even managed a little laughter. For a few precious moments, we forgot about dying. But the illusion of normality was soon shattered. Pine's family complained that I was too Tutsi and would put everyone in danger if the house was searched. Odile explained that Bosco was protecting us, but they were still unhappy.

An uneasy truce ensued, but after we had been there for a week, Munyangabo and Lionel (the head of the other family) had a blazing row about me. As if on cue, Bosco turned up. I was still a problem. He told me to put Roger on my back. David was to stay with Munyangabo.

Patricie was very worried about my safety – and so was I. As I left, I whispered my goodbyes adding, 'I think that this time they are really going to go ahead with it.'

Bosco drove into the city centre, past St Famille. To my surprise we stopped outside a photographer's shop where Bosco arranged for me to be photographed. Then, clutching the images, he disappeared into a nearby building. A few minutes later he returned holding a piece of paper. It featured my name, photograph and a note saying that I had lost my ID card. There was no mention of my ethnic group.

Illuminée, from now on you must think of yourself as Hutu. Can you do that?'

'Oh it will never work. Look at me!' I protested.

'Illuminée, I am trying to help you. You must give it a go,' pleaded Bosco.

Reluctantly I agreed, and we headed back to Munyangabo's house. There was no sign of Odile and Pine. Bosco explained that they had moved to another house, and that I was to join them with Roger and David. I was very sad to have to leave Munyangabo and Patricie; however I had no option but to follow Bosco's instructions.

Bosco showed me my room in the new house and explained that I would be given the same food as Odile and Pine. Later he brought me two sets of clothes and a pair of shoes. This new hiding place had a major disadvantage. It was a drop-in centre for the Interahamwe, who would sit drinking and smoking a few feet from me, with only a thin wall to divide us. Bosco warned me that I must stay in the room. If I was questioned, I was to show my ID paper and explain that my father was a Hutu and my mother a Tutsi.

I was very grateful that Roger continued to be such a placid baby. He was very quiet and never cried. I began to fear that he was permanently disabled and unable to talk. He seemed unnaturally happy to live on his diet of sugar and water. David was more trouble, but fortunately he looked Hutu, so did not arouse any suspicions with the Interahamwe.

After a few days Bosco came to see me. By now it was the beginning of July. He told me that he had received orders to leave Kigali and head for Zaire.

'I cannot marry you. I have done everything I can to keep you safe, Illuminée. If Odile and Pine have to leave they will take you with them.'

With that my guardian angel was gone. Why did this killer help me? I had asked for an explanation. Bosco told me that he had recognised me. He knew of John's prowess as a driving instructor, and he had also heard of my brother when Eustache was working for the Red Cross. But this was hardly a strong enough reason for him to put such an effort into solving his 'problem'.

Perhaps Rurangwa told Bosco about John and asked him to protect John's wife and son. Or possibly Bosco was just sickened by the killing – and I was the lucky one who appeared on his radar at the right time. Whatever his motivation, I will be eternally grateful for what this man did to save us from Rwanda's nightmare.

Chapter twenty two

July 4 – Flight

Faced with the UN's delay in sending troops, but also concerned about its image as a former arms supplier of the Habyarimana regime, France announced on June 15 that it would intervene to stop the killing. The UN Security Council gave its blessing and on June 22 French troops entered Rwanda from Zaire. While intending a wider intervention, confronted with the RPF's rapid advance across Rwanda, the French set up a "humanitarian safe haven" in the south west corner of Rwanda.

On July 4, the RPF led by the current president, Paul Kagame – captured Kigali and Butare. The government collapsed and the RPF declared a ceasefire. As soon as it became apparent that the RPF was victorious, an estimated two million Hutus fled to Zaire (now the Democratic Republic of Congo). These refugees included many who have since been implicated in the massacres.

The noise of battle was almost continuous at the end of June and beginning of July, with the RPF increasing its stranglehold on the remnants of the FAR in Kigali. The irony of my situation was not lost to me – a Tutsi, protected by Hutus in a city about to be liberated by a Tutsi-led army.

On July 4, we were told that the FAR had capitulated to the victorious RPF in Kigali.

Pine, as a member of the Interahamwe, but with Tutsi connections, faced a dilemma – flight and exile, or staying behind and gambling on his Tutsi relatives keeping him safe.

He chose to head for the hills and Zaire, along with 2,000,000 other Hutus. Terrified by stories of alleged RPF atrocities, they were almost force-marched from their villages by their local 'Hutu Power' leaders and Interahamwe. The Interahamwe were to continue this domination of their fellow villagers in the refugee camps, as they controlled the distribution of food and relief supplies.

I had no choice. My fate was in Odile and Pine's hands. If I had stayed, I would have made a very obvious statement of support for the RPF and would probably have been killed on the spot. So we left the house and headed west out of the city towards Mount Kigali. Thankfully we met up with Munyangabo and his family and were able to walk with them. Pine carried David, and I, as usual, had Roger strapped to my back.

It was raining very heavily as we joined the hordes of people making their way towards the hills. We climbed the steep slopes; my legs hurt, my heart pounded and my stomach churned with anxiety. Children were screaming and the sounds of gunfire echoed all around us as the RPF encountered last-ditch resistance from the old order.

The Interahamwe were no longer manning the roadblocks. But mobile death squads were working through the crowds picking on any Tutsis caught up in the throng. I am sure that nobody felt safe in the confusion. With the crowds on constant alert, fearing that the RPF would attack, there was also the danger of being knocked over and killed in a stampede.

It was very difficult to keep our group together. Malayika, who was Munyangabo's nine year-old daughter, kept close to me. But we lost sight of her parents and by the time we arrived at the top of Mount Kigali we had become separated from Pine, Odile, David and the rest of the party.

Three soldiers appeared out of the mist. I assumed that they were members of the retreating FAR. As they approached us, I noticed that the soldiers were not speaking Kinyarwanda, but were talking to people in a mixture of English and Swahili. Then 10 more soldiers appeared, very dark skinned, with long slender noses. I realised that this was the RPF.

This should have been a moment of great joy, my deliverance from three months of suffering. But by now I trusted no one, and could not accept what was happening at face value. I suspected that these Tutsi-looking men were 'Hutu Power' spies in disguise. Any relief I felt had to compete with the worry of losing David.

One of the soldiers tried to calm me down with reassurances that David would be safe.

'Where is your husband?' he wanted to know.

'He is dead.'

'How many members of your family have been killed?'

'I do not know.'

I had hardly had time to reflect on the impact of the Genocide on my family. Calnie had been mentioned by my old school 'friend', when he took me to the roadblock to be killed. But what of my mother, other sisters, Eustache, Esther and Innocent and John's family? Roger and I could be the only ones left.

The RPF tried to quell the anxiety of the crowd. We were told that they were not going to kill anyone. Everybody should turn round and head home. The RPF was keen to share power with Hutus. The planners and key players of the Genocide would be brought to justice, but there would be no revenge killings or reprisals against ordinary Hutus. This was the message of unity that the soldiers were trying to relay to the terrified masses on Mount Kigali.

The crowd began to turn round. We walked down to a clearing where hundreds of people were sitting on the ground. The soldiers were checking everyone for guns and grenades, trying to ensure that members of the Interahamwe did not quietly slip back into Kigali.

I was exhausted and preoccupied with David. But I realised that this was a significant moment. For the first time since April 7, I could allow myself a glimmer of hope. Although my milk had dried up, Roger seemed bright and healthy. We were on our way 'home' and would not have to cope with being refugees in Zaire.

We sat in the clearing until early evening, when one of the soldiers made a sign with his hand, indicating that he wanted to talk to me.

'Where do you come from?' he asked.

'Kigali'.

'No, madame, which district do you come from?'

'I was brought up in the village of Gacuriro.'

He then asked me about what had happened to me during the Genocide. I explained that my husband had died and that I had no home to go to. After a while he reached into his pocket and handed over 5,000 Rwandan francs.

'Madame, you are going to have a hard life. Take this money and buy some sugar for the baby.'

I took the money, thanked him and returned to where I had been sitting.

'Maybe I will see you again,' he called. I did not reply.

At around 10pm we were ordered to walk further down the hill to spend the night at a school in the Nyamirambo district. Our progress was very slow. Occasionally soldiers would appear out of the dark and shine torches in our faces. We passed through a RPF checkpoint where everyone was searched for weapons. I kept asking about David, but was only given a vague promise that he would be safe.

We arrived at St Andrews High School at around 1am, only to discover that there was no room for us in the building. I spotted a man in his 50s with two young men who were rolling out a carpet in an area set aside for newcomers outside the school. The older man asked me if I would like a cup of tea. These were words from better times.

'I am extremely thirsty and would love some tea', was my eager response. He went into the school and came back with a drink, inviting Roger and me and Malayika, who was still with me, to share their carpet. A little later people came round handing out maize bread. I began to relax a bit, but had to attend to Malayika, who was crying about her missing parents.

'Maybe I will not see them again. But at least I am not alone,' she said.

I promised that we would search for them tomorrow. I knew that I had lost David on Mount Kigali, and feared that I would never see him again. Despite my sadness I curled up on the carpet and fell asleep. It was the first time in 100 days that I would face the morning without fearing that it would be my last.

Chapter twenty three

Safety?

By the end of the Genocide on July 18, some two million Hutus had fled to neighbouring countries, notably to refugee camps in Zaire. There were also reprisals against Hutus who were alleged to have participated in the holocaust.

On July 19 the RPF set up an interim government of national unity, promising all refugees a safe return to Rwanda. Pasteur Bizimungu, a Hutu, was inaugurated as president, and RPF commander Paul Kagame became vice president – eventually becoming president when Bizimungu resigned in March 2000. Another Hutu, Faustin Twagiramungu, became prime minister.

We camped at St Andrews School for a fortnight. Then we were told by the RPF that all families had to move from the school to some nearby houses that were empty. Kigali was now fully under the RPF's control, so they deemed it safe to move us on.

Fighting continued for some time in the west, and for the next two years, the new government had to deal with regular border raids from the Interahamwe, based in the refugee camps in Zaire. The army finally invaded Zaire in 1996 to forcibly close down the camps. The invasion proved the trigger for the downfall of President Mobutu's regime. The 'Hutu Power' movement still exists in the Congo, now called Forces Démocratiques de Libération du Rwanda (FDLR), but no longer seems to be a real threat to President Kagame's Government.

I was glad to be leaving the cramped, smelly school, but I was very apprehensive. I did not feel physically or mentally strong enough to fetch water and hunt for food. Kigali was in a terrible state. There were bodies everywhere and it was possible that my house would still contain its murdered occupants. I was not sure whether I was ready to face this step back to 'normality'.

Fortunately I teamed up with two widows called Emma and Chantal. Chantal had known John. She had a three year-old son and a brother with her. Emma had lost most of both her arms when the Interahamwe threw a bomb at her house that had killed her husband. Together we moved to a spacious house that had belonged to someone in the Hutu government. Water was available, and we were able to gather together household items from abandoned houses. But the atmosphere was tense: there were fights over furniture and house 'ownership'. Everyone was on the lookout for food. Some supplies were available from the school, and the RPF occasionally distributed rations.

Because I was looking after Roger, I spent most of the time in the house, doing the cooking. This suited me, as I was very nervous and found it difficult to trust my new neighbours. Sharing a house with strangers was also a new experience. It was something that I would not have particularly enjoyed before the Genocide.

All around the neighbourhood there were grisly reminders of our recent history. A group of prostitutes had lived in one of the houses. The Interahamwe had murdered them, just before the flight to Zaire. Most had been beheaded. Their body parts were lying in the street, with ripped clothes covered in dried congealed blood. The smell was indescribable. It was with you all the time. I never got used to it. But at least the fighting was over, and despite the dead bodies and the terrible losses that people had suffered, there was a growing sense of euphoria among many survivors. There was a dance at the school one night – a celebration of life.

People were saying, 'Peace has come again. We can restart our lives.'

Some women who had lost husbands agreed to marry RPF soldiers. They were treated like liberating heroes. The women decided that marriage made both practical and pragmatic sense. This was a ready-made future at a time when all the certainties in their lives had vanished. However, it was no more than a contract. The women were protected in return for cleaning, cooking and sex and hoped for some love and tenderness.

The most comforting sight was the regular RPF patrol, checking for rogue members of the Interahamwe. One evening in August I was hanging out the washing when a group of soldiers passed on their rounds. Their appearance coincided with a coughing fit, and I was doubled up in agony. Since the end of the Genocide, I had a developed a very bad chest, was coughing all the time and had lost a lot of weight. I began to think that I had contracted Aids and that the decline in my health was linked to my rape.

The leader of the group came over to talk to me. He asked why I had not been to the high school to get medication, and offered to send a young boy round later with some tablets. I thanked the soldier, who was true to his word, and arranged for the pills to be delivered. Later that afternoon, the soldier returned. It transpired that he was a captain in the RPF and, to confirm his status, eight adolescent bodyguards accompanied him.

The bodyguards remained outside while the Captain, who was wearing a gun and grenades on his belt, entered the house.

'Madame, will you share a beer with me?' was his opening gambit.

'I do not drink,' was my reply. He was trying to be friendly, but I was not keen on his attention.

'Madame, I am here to ask you to be my wife.'

This was the last thing I wanted to hear. 'I am sorry – I do not want to marry you. But please do not take this personally as I have no desire to get married at the moment.'

'Why not? I will look after you, help you rebuild your life.'

'I lost my husband three months ago. I do not want another man. Can you help bring him back?'

The Captain was surprised by my response. But he remained friendly, and after a short while he departed with his entourage.

After he had gone, Chantal and Emma said that they could not understand me. The Captain was an important person. He had a career, money, and could give me protection and a nice house. It would be a new life for Roger and myself. How could I ignore him? But I said that I was not interested. It was far too soon to welcome a new man into my life.

The Captain was obviously not going to take 'no' for an answer. He returned at 9pm. This time he was more discreet and just had one acolyte. We sat chatting for a while in the living room. Then, after a while, my housemates said that they were going to head off to bed. This was the moment that I had been dreading.

The Captain followed me to my bedroom. In Rwanda, it is considered impolite for anyone to enter a woman's bedroom unless he is the man of the house. But the Captain was clearly too 'important' to observe such courtesies.

I had a tiny room. Roger was sleeping on a small bed beside mine. Without further ado, the Captain took his gun out of its holster, placed it on the bedside table, undressed and climbed into bed. I remained silent while this was going on. Although I had suspected his motives, I was not prepared for this level of brazenness.

'Come to bed,' he said.

'I will not go to bed with you,' was my reply.

'Do you think I am ugly?'

'That is not the point.'

'Come to bed.'

'No'

'I have a gun.'

'Yes, I can see that you have a gun.'

'Do you know that I can kill you?'

This was not an empty threat. There were rumours circulating that women who had refused to sleep with RPF soldiers had allegedly been shot. How ironic; I had survived three traumatic months during which I had avoided the Interahamwe's machetes, and here was one of my 'liberators' threatening to kill me because I would not go to bed with him.

'I know that you can kill me,' I replied. 'But if I am to die, kill this child first, because I am sure that you will not want to look after him when I am gone.'

I meant these words. I was furious at this man's bullying arrogance.

The Captain's mood thawed. 'Look. Madame: I will care for you and your son. I have a newsagent's shop in Kampala [Uganda]. I will give you anything you like.'

My experience with Interahamwe interrogators had given me the strength to deal with this man. 'This is my bedroom. I do not want you in here. If you care for me, why do you threaten me? How do you know that I do not have a terrible disease? You have heard me coughing. Look, my body is very thin.'

Roger slept on as we argued into the early hours. I was beginning to feel sorry for the Captain's young bodyguard, who was no doubt shivering outside. The Captain finally gave up at 4am. 'Madame, I do not understand you. How long will you mourn your husband?'

'I do not know. But three months is not enough time.'

The next morning I outlined the events of the night before to Chantal and Emma.

Chantal reacted angrily. 'I do not understand you. Do you realise how difficult life will be on your own?'

'I have no idea how difficult my life will be,' I replied. 'But I will be happier taking my chances than diving into a marriage with someone I do not like, just for the sake of a few possessions.'

Chantal dismissed my argument with an irritated wave. Soon after she took her chance and married a soldier. I do not blame her or any of the women who married in haste. We are all different. My first priority was to find out if any of my family had survived.

Chapter twenty four

Reunited in grief

At first, some Hutus in the Zaire refugee camps admitted their role in the killings, or even boasted of it. But within a year they had realised that such admissions were risky. By the end of 1995 it was hard to find anyone who would acknowledge there had been a Genocide at all; they referred only to civil war and, possibly, some massacres.

In the West it was still not accepted that in Rwanda deliberate extermination had been carried out for political reasons, to hold and keep power – a process that had been used before elsewhere and could be recognised. Although the exact number killed in the Genocide is still unknown, it is estimated that at least 800,000 people were killed during the 100 days of slaughter. Among the dead were three quarters of Rwanda's total Tutsi population.

All over Kigali people were trying to find out what had happened to their relatives during the mayhem of the previous three months. The only source of information was word of mouth. By tapping into the 'grapevine', it was possible to gather snippets of information.

Thousands of displaced Tutsis like Chantal and myself, and others from mixed Hutu/Tutsi families like Emma, were living in abandoned houses. This meant it was very difficult to make contact with family and friends. We had to be patient, and relied on lucky breaks.

Kigali was a very strange place in August 1994. The city had been drained of its Hutu population; most had fled to Zaire. Tutsi survivors were struggling to rebuild shattered lives. At the same time we had to cope with the arrival of thousands of émigré Tutsis. The Rwandan Diaspora was on the move, returning from Burundi, Tanzania and Uganda.

Some Tutsi survivors resented the special treatment often afforded to these prodigal sons and daughters. Survivors were liable to be moved on to accommodate RPF families and friends. Although I agreed with the general thrust of the RPF's policy to encourage Rwandan exiles to return, I still felt that the treatment of those who survived the 'Hutu Power' killing fields was sometimes insensitive.

Throughout the Genocide I had always had a nagging feeling that Roger and I were the only ones left; that Mum, Eustache and my sisters had all died. Then one day I met a soldier who knew Eustache.

'Have you heard anything of my brother?' I asked.

'Eustache, Yes! As far as I know he is alive and living in Kacyiru [a Kigali district]. He has a job as a driver for the RPF.

I could not believe what I was hearing. It would not sink in. I rushed back to our house and shouted at Emma and Chantal. 'He is alive. He is alive. My brother is alive!'

I composed myself, fastened Roger to my back and headed across the city to find the family that I thought had been destroyed. After several fruitless calls at houses in Kacyiru, I spotted an army post and went up to ask if they knew of Eustache.

'You are looking for Eustache Twagirayezu? Who are you, Madame?'

'I am his sister. I have not seen him since the beginning of the Genocide. I was told that he lives near here.'

After a short discussion, they arranged for a soldier to take me to his house. We walked together for a few minutes, then the soldier pointed to a small tumbledown dwelling.

'There, he lives there.'

I thanked the soldier and, trembling, walked towards the house. I went in unannounced and came across an ordinary little domestic scene. It was a miracle – the house, furniture and food. It was as if life had always been this way.

There was Eustache's wife Odile with their son Guis Karekezi. And there too was my mother! I burst into tears.

My mother shouted, 'Illuminée!' and raced towards me. We wept and hugged. My mother met the grandchild she thought that she would never see. After this happy reunion, we sat down to tell our stories.

Mum and Berencille had survived thanks to the RPF detachment based in Kigali at the outbreak of the Genocide. The RPF had been allowed to have a token force in the capital while the power-sharing talks were taking place. The detachment was based at Nyarutarama, about 20 minutes walk from our family house. They quickly secured the local area and protected Tutsi families. Berencille, her husband Kayizeri and their children Kayizeri, Shimwa, Yvona and Muhine, along with Mum, were moved to safety in Byumba, an RPF stronghold in northern Rwanda.

My half brother Kayitani was also saved. He had gone to see how Mum was coping very early in the Genocide, and had been attacked by the Interahamwe and left for dead. Mum nursed him back to health. Ironically the Genocide brought them closer together, as Kayitani never had much time for Mum after she married Dad.

Sadly his son, Niyonshuti, had not survived. Niyonshuti lived with us during his teenage years after Kayitani and his first wife Cecille had parted. Both Cecille and wife number two, Mariana, were alive. But Niyonshuti's wife was to die of a broken heart after the Genocide.

Kayitani's daughter Brigitte was also alive. In 1992 she had fallen in love with a Hutu called Alfred. They lived together and Brigitte fell pregnant. Sadly the relationship went through a difficult patch and Brigitte returned to Kayitani's house, where she gave birth to her daughter, Giselle. Brigitte and Giselle were still with Kayitani at the beginning of the Genocide. Alfred, who worked as an agronomist and was well connected in government circles, sent an Interahamwe troop to collect his partner and daughter. They fled to Zaire and returned at the end of the Genocide. Alfred was not a killer, and was able to pick up his old job. He has prospered under the RPF-led regime.

My sister Drocelle had been well positioned during the Genocide, as she was still living with Jerome and Josephine. Jerome, who was Hutu, had nothing to do with the killers and used his money and power to protect his Tutsi wife and 'ward'.

Mum and Berencille had met up with Delphine, Calnie's eight year-old daughter, at Byumba. She told them what had happened to her family. Jean Bosco and Calnie lived near the German radio station with their four children. They thought that being close to a European presence would keep them safe: what they had not considered was that their house was also close to a FAR barracks. Very early in the Genocide the Interahamwe came for John Bosco. He had been imprisoned in the early 1990s and was obviously a marked man. He was never seen again.

Calnie, wondering what to do to protect her four children, headed for the German radio station. Most of the local Tutsis had gone there. But hopes of safety were short-lived as the Interahamwe attacked, killing people with axes and raping the women. Poor Calnie was beaten savagely, and lay dying for two days. The killers ignored her pleas for water, and she passed away in front of her children.

Delphine was taken away by a helpful stranger and, miraculously, was transferred to Byumba. Calnie's youngest daughter, Marie Grace, who was about four at the time, was later discovered in an orphanage in Byumba, and now lives with Berencille. Her two other children, Kamimi and Louis, who were aged five and four respectively, died in a terrible way. They were stoned to death along with a group of children who were trying to escape from Kigali. The news about Calnie was heartbreaking. She had worked hard all her life and was a wonderful mother and sister. She did not deserve to die in such savage circumstances.

Delphine finished her education after the Genocide, then emigrated to Norway. She and her boyfriend, Maurice, have a little daughter called Audrey Ingabire.

Eustache and the family were living in a house vacated by Hutus bound for Zaire, but his oldest child, Mandela, was missing. Eustache's Hutu friend, Nshuti, had taken him to Zaire. Fortunately Mandela later returned in good health. Nshuti was the friend who had loaned Eustache a flat in Kigali city centre after the CDR 'called'.

Eustache had managed to escape from the killers by heading to Kigali's Red Cross compound in the middle of the night. Odile and Guis followed later. The area was soon taken by the RPF, and all Tutsis in the Red Cross compound were saved.

My brother was out doing his RPF driving job when I arrived. When he got home at 2am he just looked at Roger and me and cried. Eustache told me that he did not want to hear my story yet, as he had heard and seen so many terrible things. I fully understood how he felt.

The following morning he had to go to work again, but asked me to stay. I decided against this, because I felt it would be too much for him if we lived in the house. In Rwanda, the man is head of the household and takes responsibility for all the women and children under his roof. Also I was still responsible for Malayika, so I felt I should get back to her. I thanked Eustache and went 'home', just happy that they were all alive.

A few days later, I had a visit from a former FAR soldier who had joined the RPF. He introduced himself as the boyfriend of one of Malayika's sisters. He explained that he had had nothing to do with the Genocide and brought news of Patricie and Munyangabo. The soldier had traced us via St Andrews High School. It transpired that Patricie and Munyangabo and their other children had also turned back on Mount Kigali, and were living in another part of the city.

The soldier said that he had come to collect Malayika and take her to her parents. I was suspicious, especially as I was dealing with a former FAR soldier, and said that I would only hand Malayika over to a relative. As it turned out I could have trusted him. Malayika's sisters soon turned up and they all had a joyous reunion. I was sad to wave goodbye to this brave little girl – we had been through so much together.

Around this time, I met my half brother Kayitani's second son, Cyuma, at St Andrews High School. He was a driver for the RPF. I asked if he knew what had happened to my cousin Esther and her husband Innocent. It seemed a lifetime since our wonderful evening together on what transpired to be the eve of the Genocide. Cyuma told me that the Interahamwe had killed Innocent, but Esther and her three daughters were alive. They had spent some time in the Hotel Mille Collines, later to be made famous by the film 'Hotel Rwanda'. She had fled to Kabuga, RPF territory in eastern Rwanda, and on to safety in Uganda.

But what of John's family? I found out that his father, Murindahabi, had been killed, and searched frantically for news of David. I had set my heart on David and Roger growing up together.

My hopes rose after I located Odile's family (the Odile who was the Tutsi 'wife' of Pine the Interahamwe killer). I learned that Odile, Pine and David had made it to Zaire, where they joined two million other refugees in the vast camps set up by aid agencies like the Red Cross. They had met up with Bosco, who by then had married and was living in a camp for soldiers. Bosco's wife looked after David, but he had died, probably from one of the epidemics that swept through the unsanitary camps.

Tragically, many innocent Hutu families were to die of cholera in the camps. One of the great ironies of the refugee exodus was that the Interahamwe controlled both the camps and the aid handouts. Television news from the BBC and CNN showed scenes from hell on the plains of Goma. It was as if the wrath of God had been visited on the Hutu people.

The Interahamwe, using their usual brand of intimidation and violence, became the beneficiaries of a vast international aid campaign, and were the arbiters of life and death in Zaire. The 'Hutu Power' leaders used the camps to deflect attention from their murderous campaign, trying to 'spin' what was happening into another Genocide. They certainly managed to twist the aid agencies round their little fingers.

The term Genocide is a political hot potato. During the '100 Days', the international community managed to refrain from declaring the situation in Rwanda as Genocide. Under the terms of international law, the United Nations was obliged to intervene in a Genocide. But if it was just a civil war or inter tribal dispute, the international community could just stand and watch.

Sadly there was a 40-year history of Hutu/Tutsi conflict in both Burundi and Rwanda. Tutsis had been attacked with regularity in Rwanda since 1959. But conversely, some 50,000 Hutu had left Burundi for Rwanda in 1988, following a Tutsi-inspired killing spree. Maybe this record of Hutu/Tutsi strife contributed to the failure of world leaders to recognise the severity of what was happening in 1994 until it was too late. Perhaps the fact that the Genocide was so well organised caught the world off its guard and left Western leaders playing catch-up as they watched the horror unfold on the TV news.

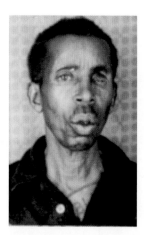

The picture on Dad's identity card. Calixte's attack permanently damaged his face.
(Chapter two Love thy neighbour)

Me aged three with my best friend, Eustache.

Mum and Dad in our backyard in the early 1970s.

John and me at home
planning our wedding.
This is the only
photograph that I have
of us together.

My only photo of our wedding on
April 3, 1994. My sister Calnie
is in the background holding a
pitcher of banana beer.

John at Aunt Azera's house.

Roger and me in 1995 with
Steve from RTV Brussels.
This was my first job after the
genocide. I worked as
an interpreter.

Cousin Esther and her daughter Babish with Mum and Roger (1995).

Bosco, the man who saved me from the Interahamwe, after his return from Zaire and release from prison.

With Roger outside our home in Bowthorpe (1997).

Roger playing for Heigham Park Rangers (October 2006).

Illuminée in London at the meeting with President Kagame (December 2006).

With Shirley Timewell and Lester Tubby in the kitchen at Gt. Yarmouth College (February 2007).

At work in the kitchen,
Gt. Yarmouth College
(February 2007).

Roger, Paul and me
– fundraising day for
Rwandan orphans at
Glynis Potter's Harambee
shop (February 2007).

Eustache, me and Drocelle (Kigali October 2006).

With Roger at
Agakera National Park
(October 2006).

Berencille, Mum and Drocelle (March 2007).

Eustache with his children: back, Moiise and Mandela and front, Benita, Benjamin and Gisa.

Eustache, Roger and me at the *Miracle in Kigali* launch, Sainsbury Centre for Visual Arts, Norwich, October 2007. Photograph, Norman Pierpoint.

Paul, me and Tony Grey at Great Yarmouth College, November 2007. Photograph, Norman Pierpoint.

Paul and me at the Rwandan launch, Hotel des Mille Collines, Kigali, July 2008.

Book signing at the Rwandan launch, Hotel des Mille Collines, Kigali, July 2008.

Paul's daughter, Rebecca, with my nephews Raymond and Claude and a huge bunch of green bananas, Rwanda July 2008.

Me with the Macmillan team at the British Embassy, Kigali, July 2008.

Me with Rev'd Norman Steer at 50 Christmas Trees in a Church, Dickleburgh, Norfolk, December 2009.

Roger on the *Africa United* set, Ruhengeri, Rwanda 2010. Photograph Nick Wall
© Pathé Productions, British Broadcasting Corporation, UK Film Council, Africa United Limited, Dudu Productions Limited and Manbury Trading (Propietary) Limited 2010.

On the red carpet at the
Africa United premiere,
Odeon, Leicester Square,
London, October 2010.

Fiona Rawlinson and
me at St Peter and St
James Church, Hereford,
November 2011.

Roger as Jumah in *Sixteen*. Photograph © Seize Films.

Roger at the RTS West of England Awards evening, March 2017. Rob Brown, Sixteen's Director, is holding the trophy. Photograph, RTS West of England.

Roger as Dadir
Hassan in BBC
drama, Informer
Photograph © Neal Street
Productions/BBC

Les Blancs,
National Theatre,
programme cover.

Roger and me with Stephen Bumfrey after
an interview on his BBC Radio Norfolk
show, January 2019.

It has been well documented that the tiny UN force in Rwanda, headed by General Romeo Dallaire, was left impotently watching people being hacked down before them. Despite Dallaire's pleadings, the UN refused to give him a mandate to intervene.

Many experts have concluded that it probably suited the Western powers to view the Genocide as Rwanda's business. The United States, in particular, was loath to put the lives of US servicemen at risk following their involvement in Somalia in 1993. If this was not Genocide, they could leave us well alone.

The French, who had been propping up the Habyarimana regime, did intervene in the later stages of the Genocide. Operation Turquoise was set up in western Rwanda. But rather than focus on the surviving Tutsi population, it allowed the Interahamwe to escape to Zaire.

In recent years, aid has poured into Rwanda from all over the world. President Clinton went on record to apologise for the lack of international intervention and has become a firm friend of the Rwandese, working hard with Bill Gates to help us overcome our Aids tragedy.

This support for Rwanda is to be applauded, but no matter how hard the international community tries to help, it cannot bring back John, his father, Azera, Festus, David, Calnie, Jean Bosco, Kamimi, Louis, Niyonshuti, Innocent and many other members of my extended family.

Chapter twenty five

Eviction

The fact that aid workers in the Zaire camps did not separate those involved in the massacres from innocent refugees angered the new government in Rwanda, who wanted to bring the guilty to trial.

The Rwandan Government tried to encourage refugees to return home from Zaire. But anyone making a move to go was likely to be killed by the Interahamwe, who controlled the camps. In August 1996, the Rwandan Army invaded Zaire to shut down the refugee camps, drive out the Interahamwe and enable the refugees to return home.

With the return of the refugees, the Government began the long-awaited Genocide trials, which had an uncertain start at the end of 1996 and inched forward in 1997. In 2001, the Government began implementing a participatory justice system, known as Gacaca, in order to address the enormous backlog of cases. Meanwhile, the UN set up the International Criminal Tribunal for Rwanda, based in Arusha, Tanzania.

Not long after our family reunion my brush with the Captain came back to haunt me.

A female RFP official visited one day when I was working in the garden. She wanted to know who lived in the house, because the RPF needed to make provisions for food and housing for all displaced Rwandese and people returning from Uganda, Tanzania and Burundi.

Three hours later, she returned with a bodyguard. 'Madame, I have been checking and believe that you are not supposed to be living in this house.'

'Why?' I replied.

'This is a big property and must be made available for people who can afford to pay a rent to live here.'

My heart sank. I was tired of constantly moving around. I knew that Emma was hoping to return to her old house and that Chantal would soon be married. It would be difficult to justify staying in the house by myself. But I was not going to give up without a fight. 'What about the other people that live here. Don't they get a say in what happens?'

'They are not here,' was her unsympathetic response. 'Look, this is going to be someone else's house. That is what the Government has ordered. Come along with us. We have another place for you.'

I had no choice. So I strapped Roger to my back – again – and we set off. We went to the neighbourhood where Stephanie (my cousin Esther's sister) lived. I thought they were going to take me to her house, but we passed by. I could see that it was already occupied. Eventually the car stopped outside a small windowless outhouse, probably used as sweet potato store.

'Would you like to live here?'

I did not reply. I just stared at her.

She then raised her voice as if I was deaf. 'Will you accept this house?'

'No, I will not accept this house.'

In the silence that followed I thought to myself. 'Why didn't I die? Have I survived just to bring up my baby in a shed?' The woman muttered to the driver in English, thinking that I could not understand. 'These Rwandans are so difficult!'

We travelled back in silence and I was dropped off at my 'home'.

Then, in the early evening, two vehicles pulled up carrying a fridge and other furniture.

I spoke to the men as they carried the items inside. 'Are they kicking me out already? Cannot they wait until I have found somewhere to live? I have a small baby.'

'Madame, you were offered a home and refused. Besides, this house is needed now.'

'Who needs the house in such a hurry?'

'We do not know his name. But he is a captain in the RPF.'

It all fitted in to place. Eviction was the price that I had to pay for resisting the advances of my newsagent Captain.

Chapter twenty six

Trying to live again

After the Genocide, Rwanda's prisons were full to bursting point with suspects awaiting trial. Thousands more were known to be among the returning refugees. Killers and survivors found themselves living side by side, sometimes (for lack of choice) in the same house. In 1996 the government surprised everyone by declaring a moratorium on arrests of those suspected of being genocidaires. The new president, Paul Kagame, broadcast messages urging Rwandans to welcome back their brothers and sisters, and to live peacefully together.

I managed to find temporary accommodation for a while, and then linked up with Mum and Drocelle. We moved to a broken-down house near Eustache in Kacyiru. All the windows had been smashed, but we did not mind. We were just happy to be together again.

Soon afterwards, my cousin Esther and her daughters came to live nearby. She took up with Oxfam again as their Rwandan director. Before the genocide she had been involved with large refugee camps at Byumba and Nyacyonga. There was no water and limited food at the camps, so Oxfam had stepped in to sort things out.

There is a Rwandan proverb, 'umwna umwe si umwana'. Roughly translated this means, 'One child is not a family.' My increasingly exasperated mother was to regularly remind me of this proverb in the months after the Genocide. Rwandan families are usually very large: six, seven or eight children is quite normal. The idea of being a single parent by choice is very unusual in our society. Many widows remarried very quickly, but I had no interest in this pragmatic approach.

Matters came to a head when Drocelle married Fideli a few months after the Genocide. They soon began producing children and now have three boys: Pacifique, Manzi and Diouf, and one daughter, Karin. I was chatting to Mum at Drocelle's wedding reception and told her that I did not think that I would marry again. Mum was very angry.

'How can you say that? You are still young, and Roger needs a brother and sister.'

I had already received several marriage proposals, and believed that I had good reasons for turning them down. First of all, I felt that it was still too soon after John's death. I had only been married for five weeks, and was not ready to consign my marriage to the past. Towards the end of 1994 I went back to Nyarutarama, the place where John had proposed. It was then that I decided that I wanted to tell the story of his death and my survival, not only to keep his memory alive but also to explain to the next generation what had happened to ordinary people during the Genocide.

Secondly, I suspected that I might be HIV positive – the legacy of the Hutu student's visit. I attributed my weight loss and persistent cough to the onset of Aids. I had kept the rape a secret from my family. Like many women, I was too ashamed to talk. I did not think that I had a life to offer anyone.

Finally, the way that I had allowed my relationship to develop with John was completely at odds with the way that I had wanted to get to know a prospective husband. It had all happened so fast. If there was to be a second time, I wanted to get to know the man and not dive head first into life with a complete stranger. I had to be careful that the person I married was not 'trouble.'

I also felt guilty about the way that I had squandered my education. My parents had wanted me to complete high school, but by falling pregnant with John I had turned my back on my unfinished schooling. So I had to be careful in future with affairs of the 'heart'.

My definition of 'trouble' included marrying soldiers. A distant relation, who was also called John, was in the RPF. When he came home he made it clear that he wanted to marry me. But I did not want an army wife's life. I wanted a husband who came home in the evening (eventually!), not someone who was always away with the army. I turned down several proposals from soldiers for this reason.

94

I was very strong in the months after the Genocide. My survivor's instinct made me protect my son and myself. I definitely had no room for another man. Of course I had to find a job. Mum was able to look after Roger and so, with Eustache's help, I set up a clothes-making business with Drocelle. We rented small premises, and for four months we struggled to make ends meet until the costs forced us to give up.

Soon after, I managed to get a month's work with a television crew from RTV Brussels. They were making a film about Genocide widows, and my job was to interpret Kinyarwanda into French. When I talked to young girls in the countryside it made me forget about my own problems. The Belgians were very complimentary, and told me how brave I was to work on a programme about the Genocide. But it was a really good experience for me, as it was the first time that I had worked with Europeans.

My search for a full-time job even saw me flirt with the idea of joining the army. I thought that it would be a good way to get rid of my anger. But a friend of my brother's called Captain Ntare managed to persuade me that it would not be a good career move.

In autumn 1995 I finally managed to get a job doing stock control and book-keeping for a drinks company run by a Tutsi widow called Victoire Mukarubuga. Her son had worked for her before the Genocide but had been killed, so she needed an extra pair of hands. I really enjoyed the job: it helped boost my confidence. Victoire was very kind to me, and sent a car to pick me up every morning and take me home in the evening.

The following summer, Oxfam gave Esther the chance to go to the University of East Anglia (UEA) in Norwich for a year to study counselling. The plan was that when she returned to Rwanda she would work for Avega, an organisation set up to support Genocide widows. Esther was very keen to go to Norwich, but was worried about her three daughters. Who would look after them while she was studying?

I felt happy and strong at the time. My job was going well with Mrs Mukarubuga, and Roger was developing wonderfully. But my family was not sure what do with me. They were sad that I would not marry – to them I seemed to be dwelling too much on the past.

Esther asked me if I would like to accompany her and work as the children's nanny. After giving it serious thought, I agreed to go to England with her. My family were delighted, and thought that the trip would be an exciting opportunity for me. But there was another reason why I was pleased to be leaving Rwanda for a while. 'They' started coming back in 1996. 'They' were the genocidaires, the men who had fled to Zaire in July 1994.

Our new RPF-led government was promoting reconciliation to end 'La Haine' and enable Hutu and Tutsi to live harmoniously. At the same time the RPF pledged to bring the architects of the Genocide to justice. Those who oversaw the planning and killing, including leading members of the Interahamwe, could expect the death sentence. But where did that leave the 'foot-soldiers' of the Genocide, who had fled to Zaire and could argue that their's was a case of kill or be killed?

Because of the scale of the Genocide, it was going to prove very difficult for the Government to track down every killer or rapist. The average Hutu who did his 'work' could expect up to seven years in prison. But as the prisons filled up, many killers hoped that they would avoid prison altogether.

Just before I left Rwanda, the RPF invaded Zaire to break up the refugee camps, leading to a mass repatriation of some 500,000 Hutus. This ended the Interahamwe's control, but brought with it huge resettlement and judicial problems. The Government introduced the local Gacaca court system for bringing lower grade killers to justice. These community courts are still working away at village reconciliation.

The possibility that genocidaires might return home and escape justice filled me with painful and powerful emotions. There were times when I wanted to kill the killers – 'an eye for an eye'. But I was also terrified that 'they' might come knocking again to finish their work. This was a key influence in my decision to give Rwanda a wide berth for a year.

Getting a passport was not easy, because the Government was wary of allowing the Interahamwe to slip through its net. Fortunately the first civil servant that I met at the passport office was a former high school colleague. He had left Rwanda after school to join the RPF. His sister, who had also been a fellow student, had been killed in the Genocide.

He was very excited to see me. 'Illuminée, how are you still alive?'

I became used to answering that question with a smile, a nod and a shrug of the shoulders. He was so pleased that I was still alive and said he would do anything to help me.

'I would like to get a passport and visa to go to the UK.'

'That is no problem, go out of this country and never come back!'

But of course I did not feel like that at the time. I thought that I would return to Rwanda after Esther had finished her year-long course. My passport and visa arrived within a week.

Chapter twenty seven

Norwich

We flew to London via Kenya on September 8, 1996. It was the first time that I had been in an aeroplane, and I was very frightened. I had never been out of Rwanda before.

As we approached the UK, I started feeling really cold. I was only wearing a thin skirt and jacket. Heathrow airport was a complete culture shock, very different to Kigali, because it was so crowded and frantically busy. Two of Esther's Oxfam colleagues, Anne MacIntosh and Sarah Wescot, came to Heathrow to meet us and drove us to Norwich.

All the houses fascinated me. I wondered how anyone remembered where they lived! The roads were terribly busy and there were no people to be seen – unlike Rwanda where everyone was on foot. I later found out that people are not allowed to walk on motorways!

We lived in a fully furnished house that belonged to the university in Bowthorpe, a suburb west of Norwich. My job was to look after Esther's three children and my own son while she was doing her course. It was all very strange. I only spoke a little English, and had to quickly adapt to shopping with British currency. My accent also made it very difficult for people to understand what I was saying. It took me a month to understand the value of a pound coin, and even longer to differentiate between all the small coins. The currency is much more straightforward in Rwanda!

I knew that I had to learn English quickly, and managed to find some afternoon lessons at the local church. Then I went to Bell School of Languages in Norwich to see if I could get on a course. They asked me where I came from, and if I had any money. I told them I had no money and was asked to fill out an application form.

My cousin was really angry that I had gone there, because I was not in Norwich to be a student. She thought that it was wrong for me to even consider a course at the language school because I had no money. But I was lucky; the language school wrote to me within a week and offered me a free place for two months. I really enjoyed my time with the other foreign students. They thought I was brilliant! The teachers were very enthusiastic and worked hard to improve our grammar. I also managed to go to Norwich City College to study English as a second language. Ten years on I still want to develop my English. It is not perfect. I love the language, and am keen to improve my written work.

The house was amazing compared to life in Rwanda, with mains sewage, water on demand and good electricity. One of the best appliances in the house was the washing machine. This was an unheard of luxury in Rwanda, and I had never encountered one before. There were no more trips down to the local river! It was also the first time I had been in a building with stairs. To begin with I was quite frightened to come downstairs, thinking I would fall over and hurt myself. Going on an escalator was something else – very scary!

All our living expenses came from Esther's Oxfam salary. I was here to look after the house and the children, and it was a great experience. Being the youngest in our family, I had never looked after children. It worked out well, but it was still exhausting at times. I felt very cold during my first winter; my ears and hands were freezing, and the cold slowed me down quite a lot. But my first snow compensated for the cold weather. I had never seen snow before and loved it. I am a little child when the snow falls!

Esther said she would never go to church again because of priests' involved in the Genocide, but I went to the local church in Bowthorpe and liked it. After I had been twice my cousin relented and joined us. They had a playgroup, and it was good for the children to mix with others. Everyone was friendly at the church but of course it was hard to communicate, as I knew very little English at the time. I still keep in touch with some people from the church and regularly play badminton on Saturday with one lady I met there, called Sally.

Because my main focus was the children, my social life was fairly limited. But I made good friends with a Spanish girl who was at Bell School and we went out together occasionally.

In February 1997 I received a letter from Drocelle telling me that Alphonse Gasasira had returned to our neighbourhood from Zaire. He was the man who had chopped off John's arms with a machete. Gasasira, like many other Genocidaires, had expected to settle down to life as before in his old neighbourhood. But all was not as he had imagined. People asked him, 'What have you done with John's arms?' Frightened that he might be attacked, he moved to live with his sister in Butare.

Ironically Gasasira prospered as a result of this move and became mayor of his village. Drocelle was, and still is, very angry with this, but I told her not to get involved. To bring someone to justice at a Gacaca court, you have to have several witnesses who will testify that they saw the murder take place. This is a difficult process. Apparently people are scared to come forward; so many families just live uneasily with the genocidaires in their community. Drocelle could have opened herself up to violence if she had pursued Gasasira to Butare.

In my heart, I knew that I could not face one of my husband's killers. It would be so difficult to go home and know that I could bump into him on the street. I was frightened. There were still a lot of killings in Rwanda. Former Interahamwe would cross from Zaire and murder people. I thought that Gasasira or one of his cronies might finish his 'work' and murder Roger and me. But it was not just the fear that stopped me returning. I decided that I wanted Roger to grow up away from the hatred, to have a chance to develop in safety and make his own mind up about his home country.

Deep inside I 'knew' that I had Aids. My time in Norwich with Esther and the children should have been a period of recovery from the Genocide. But I was constantly troubled by dark thoughts. I had convinced myself that I was not a 'true' survivor. I was under sentence of death thanks to the disease that was taking hold of my skinny frame.

I was too afraid to have an Aids test. 'There is no point,' I told myself. 'I will just wait until I know that my health is failing. Hopefully by then I will be in a position to make arrangements for Roger.'

I had taken an Aids test in Rwanda and experienced the dread involved. Esther had put doubts in my mind about John, suggesting that he had been with lots of girls and that I should use a condom to be safe. I was always very open with John and told him what she had said. 'Ok, let's go and have an Aids test,' was his instant response. Although I agreed, I would still have preferred to have been in blissful ignorance. I had to cope with the wait, then the trip to the surgery to get the results and, on arrival, scanning the nurse's face to see if it revealed any news.

Thank God, the results put us in the clear. But this time it was different. I knew I was at risk. How many other women had the Hutu student raped? Rape had been a routine part of the Interahamwe's armoury. I told myself that the student must have been infected. The evidence was overwhelming. I was skinny and could not put on weight, and my immune system was not functioning properly. I was constantly picking up minor infections which troubled me for a long time. Soon I would become another Genocide statistic.

It was a big step to consider staying in the UK. I would be leaving my family behind in Rwanda and starting a new life in Norwich. In Bowthorpe we had been living in a kind of 'mini Rwanda', but living by myself I would have to learn very quickly about life in the UK. I knew I would have to fully adapt to the culture if I was to settle here successfully.

I discussed applying for asylum with my cousin, and of course all the negative things about living in a strange country thousands of miles from home came to the surface. But my brother was very happy to hear that I wanted to stay in Norwich. I was never able to tell him everything that was going on in my head, including the fear that I would die from Aids. Nevertheless, he recognised that I had a lot of inner turmoil and that being away from Rwanda might prove to be a new beginning for me.

Eustache's support kept me going as I tackled life as single mum in Norwich. It was very hard for my mother and my sisters, especially Mum as she was worried about how I was going to cope on my own in this strange city. She realised how tough it would be for me on my own.

It was horrible when my cousin returned to Rwanda. She hired a car to drive down to Heathrow, so we said our goodbyes in Norwich. Roger was very unhappy when his cousins left. But I knew in my heart that this was a good opportunity for him; it would give us the chance to develop a new life well away from the horrors and scars of the Genocide.

Esther started working with the Genocide widows. But she only did that job for one year, as she fell in love with a German pastor. They married and she moved with her children to Germany. She has put her counselling skills to good use there working with refugees.

The Minister of Bowthorpe Church, Eric Maple, and his wife Valerie helped me begin the asylum process. They invited me to stay with them for the first week after Esther had gone, to ensure that I had some company.

Looking back, I realise how badly prepared I was for the challenges that lay ahead.

Chapter twenty eight

Becoming British

Ten years after the Genocide ended more than 11% of Rwanda's population were living with HIV or Aids. The average life expectancy in Rwanda is 49 years, and one in five children die before they reach the age of five. (Source: SURF Survivors' Fund/UNICEF)

My lawyer, Janet Dalgliesh, took me through the asylum process. I did not have to do much. We had one visit to the Home Office in London, and towards the end of 1998 I was given leave to remain indefinitely in the UK. I had to wait four years before I could apply for British citizenship which was approved in 2002, so now I have both UK and Rwandan passports.

The Umbrella Housing Association gave us our first home and helped fund the rent. It was one-room accommodation for single parents on Unthank Road in Norwich. I found it very difficult living there. That was when my depression started to kick in. The children called Roger a monkey, and it was very noisy and frightening. We were the only black people living there. It was the first time that we had to cope with racism.

Fortunately we had a very good social worker called Rosemary Horner, who took what we told her seriously. She wanted to know who had called Roger names and managed to move us on, so we only had to live on Unthank Road for five months. Our next home, which was provided by the same housing association, was about two miles away on Dereham Road. I was so pleased to be away from all the drinking, swearing and shouting that went on all through the night at our previous accommodation.

Of course at this time I still thought that I would eventually die from Aids.

I never went for a test – what was the point? I just wanted Roger to be safe in England, and I would die when my time came. As a result, I never talked to anyone about what had happened to me in the Genocide. But six months after Esther left I began feeling really ill. I could not eat or drink.

Then I stopped sleeping, and began hallucinating. Images from the Genocide kept flashing in front of my eyes. I stayed in bed all the time and was in a terrible condition.

Fortunately, a friend realised that I was in a bad way and telephoned for a doctor. He took one look at me and sent for an ambulance. At the hospital I was immediately put on a drip.

I had to stay in hospital for three months, while foster carers looked after Roger. The medical staff thought that I was a child at first, because I had lost so much weight. I realised that I could no longer remain silent about the Genocide and my hallucinations. So I told them my story and explained that I had been raped.

My doctor said that I needed an Aids test. He explained that a positive test did not mean that I was necessarily going to die, as there had been major advances in the treatment of the disease. After a week the test results came through: I was given the all clear. My immediate response was, 'Are you sure?'

The news traumatised me. I had been expecting to die, and had been living in a kind of limbo. Now I realised I was going to live I somehow had to come to terms with the Genocide and plan a future for Roger and myself. I could not cope with this realisation, and was literally struck dumb. The trauma – made worse by the fact that I was very dehydrated – was terribly serious. I could not face anything red, and the smell of meat made me think of dead people. My Genocide experiences were constantly with me. It was as if I were playing the lead role in my own horror film.

Thankfully I had a wonderful therapist called Stephen Christianson, who gradually coaxed me back to life. We communicated by writing in French, because what English I had learned was lost as I fought with my Rwandan demons. Stephen was a fantastic support, slowly building up my confidence and encouraging me to talk about the Genocide. He told me about post-traumatic disorder, and this seemed to make sense to me.

Depression was an unknown concept when I was young in Rwanda. But now, having survived the Interahamwe and the threat of Aids, I had another battle on my hands – mental illness. Sometimes I did not want to talk, but Stephen was very patient with me. Between 1998 and 2000 I was hospitalised four times. Triggers from everyday life would plunge me back into the darkness of the Genocide. I was also on anti-depressants, which made my weight balloon and contributed to my misery!

I found Bonfire Night in November particularly difficult. The noise of fireworks, especially the sound of bangers thrown by youngsters in the street, sounded like gunfire. This would throw me back to the Kigali of 1994. Thankfully nobody ever knocked on my door wearing masks at Halloween 'trick or treating' – I would not have been able to handle it.

Stephen supported me through this difficult period. He arranged for a special memorial garden to be planted at a church in Costessey, near Norwich; a place where I could go to remember John and Calnie.

Around this time Bosco wrote to me out of the blue. When he returned from Zaire, he had been put in prison for his role in the Genocide. On his release he lived in the same neighbourhood as Patricie and Munyangabo. I heard from Patricie that he was making enquiries about me, so I gave her permission to give Bosco my email address. Bosco's writings were full of his religious beliefs. He said that he was very sorry that David had died in the refugee camp. He went on to say I was a brave woman and that he would pray for Roger and me to have a nice life. Bosco could so easily have killed me during the Genocide. It is a miracle that he decided to leave his gun in its holster.

After my first spell in hospital, I spent about five months at home recuperating. I knew I needed to explore the outside world again. Roger was now at school, so did not need my continuous attention. It was time to start looking for work.

Chapter twenty nine

Working frustration

How does the only Rwandan in Norwich get a job? I had no recognised qualifications. My education had been put on hold when I fell pregnant, and was effectively terminated by the Genocide.

My first job was making beds and working as a cleaner at the YMCA. But I soon found out that if I earned a small amount of money, my benefits would be stopped. The challenge was to find a job that would pay enough to replace my benefits and at the same time be flexible enough for me to be at home for Roger.

I lasted six months at the YMCA, then decided that probably the best way to improve my experience and make me more attractive to employers was to do voluntary work. So I went along to Meridian East, a Norwich-based charity that helps people with mental health problems back to work. I became Meridian East's voluntary book-keeper for two years, working up to four days a week. Then they arranged for me to do a residential care course. But the only work that I could get was on a shift basis, which did not help with looking after Roger.

Roger was progressing very well at school. He had no memory of Rwanda and, as result, Norwich was home. His first language became English rather than Kinyarwanda, and he lapped up British culture. I talked to him in Kinyarwanda at home to try and ensure he had an understanding of his native tongue, but soon realised that I could develop my English with Roger's help!

Roger fell in love with football almost as soon as he could walk and, from when he was four, I made sure he was involved in organised football coaching and teams. He has developed into a very good striker and now plays for City of Norwich School, Heigham Park Rangers and also a local church team. So life is often just football, football, football. He has been to watch Norwich City play quite a few times, thanks to the generosity of parents of his Heigham Park team-mates, and has even had trials for the Norwich City Academy, but has been told that he needs to fill out a bit more before they can consider him. But it is Liverpool that has captured his heart. He became a fan of the club when the black striker, Emile Heskey was playing there.

But back to work. My next port of call, early in 2003, was Norwich and Norfolk Racial Equality Council. Perhaps they could help me get work? I was welcomed with open arms, but again it was as a volunteer.

In February that year I was invited by the Rwandan Embassy to fly to Geneva for the day, to meet Rwanda's president Paul Kagame. The Embassy keeps in touch with expatriates in the UK. As a result I have been to London to meet Rwandan ambassadors Rosemary Museminali and Claver Gatete soon after they were appointed, and also heard Paul Kagame speak in December 2006.

The meeting in Geneva was for all Rwandans living in Europe. There had been rumours that people returning to Rwanda were being murdered, and Paul Kagame wanted to put the record straight. After his speech, there was an open question session. I was lucky to be selected. It was the first time I had ever spoken to anyone in the Rwandan government, and I found that Paul Kagame was very approachable.

I had prepared three questions for him. I wanted to suggest that Rwanda needed a truth and reconciliation process like South Africa; to ask for more counsellors to be trained to help traumatised Rwandans, and to urge him to explore how the cycle of blame and hatred could be broken in our country. In the end I only had time to talk to him about counselling. He agreed that more counselling was a good idea, and I encouraged him to send people to the UK to get trained – as Esther had been – and also to recruit European counsellors to work in Rwanda.

There were a lot of questions about the alleged murders. Kagame said that he was not aware of a problem, and emphasised that if we wanted to return to live in Rwanda we had nothing to fear. He also encouraged us to do business with Rwanda to help the country's economy.

I was filmed talking to Paul Kagame and appeared on a TV news report in Rwanda. A friend saw the film and had a big surprise! I have yet to see it and would love to get a copy as a souvenir of my meeting with the President. It was a day to remember.

Chapter thirty

Return to Rwanda

In August 2003 Paul Kagame received 94 per cent of the vote in Rwanda's first presidential election since the Genocide.

Meeting Paul Kagame inspired me to organise a Rwandan Genocide Remembrance Day in Norwich in April 2003. Even though I was the only Rwandan in the city, I decided that it was important to officially commemorate those who were murdered in 1994. I contacted the Rwandan ambassador, Rosemary Museminali, who offered to send Makuza, her First Counsellor, to speak at the event. She also provided Rwandan dancers to entertain guests at the reception.

The day began with a service at my local church, Holy Trinity, which was attended by 100 people including the Chief Constable of Norfolk. We lit candles to remember the Genocide victims. This was followed by a reception at the International Club. Norwich and Norfolk Racial Equality Council provided a car for the day, and Dr Eshetu Wondimagegne of Norfolk African Community Association helped set up the reception.

I cooked a Rwandan meal for everyone at the International Club. After lunch I made a speech and was followed by Makuza, who congratulated me for organising the day. He said that it was a very brave thing for me to do as a survivor, especially as I was the only Rwandan living in Norwich. He also talked about what the Rwandan government was doing to rebuild the country.

Although the day was well received, I do not feel that I can organise another public remembrance. It is time for me to try to move on from the Genocide. I want to enjoy my life and put the horrors behind me. I will continue to think about John, Calnie and the other members of my family who died – but I will do this in private at my garden of remembrance in Costessey.

This book is also an important element of moving on from the Genocide. I can put the book and the Genocide physically and metaphorically on the shelf, and can open the pages whenever I feel the need.

Many people in Rwanda cannot cope with the April anniversary. Hospitals overflow with traumatised survivors. There are those in Europe who feel the same way. I did my best publicly in 2003 to show how I feel about 1994. It will never leave me. Of course, I would be very happy to take part if someone else organized a remembrance day!

BBC Look East covered the event in 2003 and contacted me the following year to see if I was going to arrange anything special for the tenth anniversary. Ten years on, it was time for me to go back to Rwanda with my new British passport. I wanted to spend time with my family on the anniversary, and also give Roger the opportunity to get to know his cousins and his country. I was only able to consider going thanks to money raised by Roger's football team.

I told the BBC that I was planning a fortnight's visit to Rwanda. The response was quite surprising: I was asked if a film crew could accompany us and make a short documentary for their 'Inside Out' series. Victoria Holden, the journalist who joined us, produced a very good film which focused on Roger's return home. It began with Roger watching a Norwich City game, then followed his progress in Rwanda: getting to know his cousins, visiting the house I shared with John, as well as Azera's house, where the imprints of John's bloodstained hands were still visible on the walls. We also went to the Gisozi Genocide Memorial and my old school, Apace College, and passed the site of Pastor Amoni's house.

The BBC film encouraged us to visit more locations than we would have done on our own. I am not sure that I would have had the courage to explore the old houses without their support. One of the saddest moments was when Roger was filmed adding a photograph of his father to the huge display at the Gisozi Memorial. I also found out that Dad's body had been reburied at Gisozi because he was a victim in 1959. The Gisozi Memorial is very powerful, a permanent reminder of the horrors of 1994. It is so important that all Rwandese children go there, so they can understand what happened to their country and help bring an end to 'La Haine'.

We stayed at my brother's house. Mum was there all the time, and it was wonderful to see all my family and friends after such a long time. We even met up with one of my teachers.

Churches like Bugesera at Ntarama that have been left as memorials, with bodies lying where they were cut down, are equally important. The 'Hutu Power' leaders deny that there was a Genocide and try to explain that they killed in defence. They blame the RPF for the Genocide. But go to a church and view the bodies, or see the bones and photographs and weapons at the Kigali memorial. These places prove to the world that this killing was planned aggression rather than a defensive act.

Rwanda was very different and changing for the better. Kigali was full of people busily going about their lives. There was sense of urgency about the country, a shared determination that Rwanda could be rebuilt. But everything is a lot more expensive, probably because they have to rely on imports, as the country's agriculture and other industries were destroyed by the Genocide and are taking time to recover.

Back in Norwich I decided that I had had enough of volunteering – I wanted paid work. So I applied to Sainsbury's, who took me on as an unpaid trainee with the promise of a job once I had enough experience. But the job did not materialise. I applied for lots of shop assistant-type jobs, but rarely received a reply.

The BBC documentary won one of the categories at the One World Media Awards. Roger and I went down to London where we met Channel 4's Jon Snow, who presented the award. The film also led to a new friendship. A lady called Glynis Potter from East Bergholt in Suffolk had seen the documentary on TV and contacted me via the BBC. She wanted to invite Roger and me to the launch of a calendar that she had produced to raise money for Kibuye Hospital.

Glynis and her friend Anne Neve had opened a shop called Harambe in Hadleigh in 2003. At first the shop mainly focused on items made by Rwandan orphans and widows, but they subsequently expanded their range of fair trade goods to include those made in other African countries and India. Harambe will soon be moving from Hadleigh to Felixstowe.

Glynis held a final fundraising day at the shop in February 2007, to raise money for Rwandan orphans. I made Rwandan lentil soup, which was given to customers in return for a donation. My soup went down very well! It was wonderful for me and my son to be involved in such a positive event for Rwanda. Soon after the fundraising day Glynis went to Rwanda to visit the orphan projects that she supports. Eustache helped her during the visit and she was also able to meet Mum. It was the first time that a friend from the UK had met my mother.

But I am jumping ahead. In autumn 2005, a new shopping mall opened in Norwich near where I live. All the stores were advertising for staff, but again I had no luck. What was wrong with me? I decided to go back to Meridian East and asked them if they could help me get work. They managed to find me part-time employment in a store restaurant, which I thought might be a stepping stone to a career in the catering industry. I enjoyed cooking, and harboured a secret ambition to open a Rwandan restaurant in Norwich.

Sadly, the restaurant job proved to be my worst work experience to date. I was told that I was going to be waitress, but instead they kept me in the kitchen just doing the washing up. I put up with this for four months, as the management promised that I would eventually be allowed out of the kitchen. But life in the restaurant turned quite nasty. I was not given any breaks and was told to keep working on the wash up. They were treating me badly: to them I was a stupid little black woman with no qualifications.

The situation made me ill and I had to take time off over Christmas. When I went back in the January they sacked me. It took me until April to get my P45.

Meanwhile, I tried to get onto a course at the University of East Anglia to develop my written and spoken English, but the Department of Employment told me that they could not give me a grant.

Being a single, black, refugee parent makes me very vulnerable. I could not have survived without the help of the health authorities and social services, but at the same time this reliance on support opens me up for unwarranted intrusion. It is as if I will always be stigmatised for having had mental health problems. But all I want is for us to get on with our lives.

My health continued to worry me. I had become wary of going to my local surgery too often, so in February 2006 friends in Brussels arranged for me to see a doctor there. He gave me a thorough check-up and some excellent medicine, which helped a lot. I did not take Roger with me and arranged for a Rwandan girl to visit for a few days to do the baby-sitting. When I returned home I was met by a woman who used to be our social worker, and the police.

112

I was accused of leaving Roger without adequate supervision and was also accused of stealing the Rwandan girl's passport. This was madness; I would not have left Roger with the girl if I had not been confident that all would be well. What made me really angry was that the 'intruders' had been going through my private papers. It was almost as if they thought that they had the right to control me.

I was very angry – I went ballistic, as you say in the UK. This was not a good move. I was handcuffed and bundled into a police car which took me to Hellesdon Hospital, our local mental health institution. I was obviously 'mad' and needed an injection to calm me down. Roger, who was terribly upset, was taken away into care.

At the hospital I protested my innocence with the medical staff. They listened to my story, agreed that there was nothing wrong with me and sent me home. But that was not the end of the incident, as it was some time before Roger returned. I had to fight for custody of my son.

What right did this social worker have to interfere with my life? I believed that I had made perfectly suitable arrangements for Roger's care. The social worker, I am sure, thought that she was acting in Roger's best interests. But did she think about me and the impact on my mental health and long-term recovery from the traumas of 1994?

My life had hit a new low. But as luck would have it, a reporter from the Norwich Evening News, Naomi Canton, contacted me to ask if she could do a story on my life as the only Rwandan refugee in the city. I agreed and talked to her about the Genocide, the problems that I had faced getting a job and my desire to get my story published.

During the winter of 2002/03, Adrian Galvin, one of the parents of Roger's football team-mates, had taped my experiences in the Genocide and had put together the core of a book which I had planned to present to President Kagame in Geneva. I did not get the chance to give the story to the President and the publishing project stalled. But I still hoped that I could find a way to produce a book, even just one copy for Roger.

Naomi wrote a good piece about the ups and downs of my life, and included an appeal for someone to help me finish my story. I waited for the phone to ring.

Chapter thirty one

by Roger Nsengiyumva

*In this chapter Roger compares Rwanda
with his life in Norwich*

I do not really think about growing up in Norwich. I can only say that it is normal. Norwich is my home. I first became 'aware' of where I was in Norwich and have no memories of my time in Rwanda. I have lots of friends in Norwich and know lots of people and feel very comfortable in the city.

My ambition is to become a professional footballer. I play for three teams and love football. Most weekends are taken up with playing football. I am a striker and am very quick and can run onto balls passed over my head or through balls along the ground – just like Robert Earnshaw or Michael Owen when he played for Liverpool.

I support Liverpool. This may seem strange as I live in Norwich. But Emile Heskey was one of the first strikers that I followed. He was playing for Liverpool at the time, so Liverpool has always been my team. I really like Stephen Gerrard as well.

Mum has told me a lot about Dad, my family, Rwanda and the Genocide. She has also done her best to ensure that I understand Kinyarwanda. I know I am in trouble when she starts speaking our native language!

It was wonderful going back to Rwanda in 2004 and meeting my family. My cousins, of course, spoke Kinyarwanda, but they are learning English at school. We managed to understand each other with a mix of English and Rwandan. If we became completely confused, we asked Mum to interpret.

I enjoyed meeting my family's friends. It was good to hear and see people from my own country. I had great fun riding on the back of my uncle's truck. But it is illegal here!

We went to the market and were buying food and came across a football that had been made with banana leaves. Once it had been kicked around a while, the leaves fell off. But I have kept it as a souvenir.

Toys, proper footballs and goals are very much out of the question. Children do not have many toys in Rwanda. We used empty shoes as goals and kicked around an empty bottle. It was great!

Kigali is a busy, big city. It is also very green with a lot of trees. Animals and insects roam around the city – so it can be quiet dangerous. I went to the toilet in Drocelle's house and a big poisonous spider appeared. I don't like insects so it was very frightening. You have to be careful with insects in Kigali because of malaria.

Life in Kigali is much tougher than in Norwich. People work harder. My uncle has a taxi business and works very long hours. He used to own a café. But he had to give it up; it was very difficult to earn an income.

But there is plenty of fresh food; sometimes in the markets you are sold the rotten fruit kept out of sight! The market can be quite a dirty and smelly place with lots of flies. But this is because of the climate.

There were a lot of children and poor people on the streets. Many of the children are orphans from the Genocide. The welfare state is not as well developed in Rwanda, but I know that the Government is trying to make things better.

It was very interesting when we were with the BBC, because we looked at the story of the Genocide. I was able to visit two of the houses where I lived with Mum soon after I was born, and also saw where Dad was killed. It was very sad going to the Genocide Memorial, looking at all the photographs of the people that had been killed. But I was pleased to be able to add a photograph of Dad to the display.

It is so important for children like me to see what happened in 1994, and for the World to understand the terrible things that happened in Rwanda. Another

Genocide must not happen. Look at Iraq, we have to learn from Rwanda's mistakes. The United Nations came to Rwanda, but they did not get involved; this was wrong. World leaders like Presidents Clinton and Mitterand should have intervened to stop the slaughter. People have short memories. We need to keep talking about the Genocide.

The best thing that I have ever done was to get my friends to watch me on TV! Second best was going down for the award for Victoria Holden's programme about us. I met Jon Snow. It was great. I love shouting at him during Channel 4 news, saying 'I know you!'

When I am older I think that I will try and help Rwanda. But I will need to be making a settled living here before I can consider getting involved.

Chapter thirty two

The future?

Although the massacres have ended, the legacy of the Genocide continues. The search for justice has been a long and arduous one.

Since 2003 the RPF has pursued a policy of releasing prisoners back into the community to solve overcrowding problems. It is currently considering repealing the death sentence, which will ease the extradition of suspected genocidaires from other countries, including Britain.

The phone did ring last April [2006]. A writer called Paul Dickson said that he wanted to help. We met at a Norwich hotel and he listened to my story. Paul went away with the work that Adrian and I had done four years earlier. Something told me that he would not let me down – perhaps it was finally my time.

My confidence increased as we developed the book project and Paul introduced me to Anthony Grey of The Tagman Press. My energy returned. I made contact with the Rwandan Ambassador, Claver Gatete, to ask for his help and began thinking seriously about getting a catering qualification.

I applied to both Norwich and Great Yarmouth Colleges and was delighted when Yarmouth offered me a place on the NVQ2 course, which began last September. I have really enjoyed learning my trade. The staff there have been so kind and friendly, particularly the two chef lecturers, Lester Tubby and David Rollins, and the learning support assistant, Shirley Timewell. It has been quite a challenge working in the training restaurant, but it is great fun.

I am keen to do an NVQ in management next, so that I am fully equipped to get a good job. And, who knows, to eventually open my own Rwandese restaurant in Norwich.

In October 2006 my mother fell ill and, worried that she might not have much time left, I decided to take Roger to Rwanda at half term. I managed to borrow the money for the trip. Fortunately Mum recovered, but I am so pleased that I made the effort to go. I stayed with Mum and spent a lot of time with her, as well as meeting all our old neighbours once again. Calixte's daughter came to see us. I used her visit to show the neighbourhood that her father's attack on Dad was long in the past, and that it was time to move on.

Eustache organised a big family outing to Akagera National Park. Sadly, global warming is having an impact on the landscape. It has become very dry, and many of the animals have left to find better grazing. However, we still had a wonderful time together – and we did see lots of baboons, who live on a diet of green bananas. Eustache also took Roger to Hotel Mille Collines for a swim in the pool – his first experience of 'Hotel Rwanda'.

Soon after we returned I started volunteering again, this time for Oxfam at their big shop on Magdalen Street in Norwich. Amazingly one of my fellow volunteers, Jill Crum, was born in Rwanda just before World War II, and spent the first 18 years of her life there. Her parents were Church of England missionaries. It is very exciting for me to be able to talk in Kinyarwanda to someone in Norwich.

One of the highlights of 2006 was an invitation from the Rwandan Embassy to attend a meeting with President Kagame. More than 600 Rwandans packed a conference room at the Royal Garden Hotel, Kensington on Sunday, December 3, to listen to their President. Paul Dickson accompanied me. However, the evening was quite a challenge for him as virtually all the speeches were in Kinyarwanda!

The Rwandan Genocide continues to be in the news. The mystery surrounding the death of President Habyarimana resurfaced towards the end of 2006. French judge Jean-Louis Bruguiere alleged that Paul Kagame, then leader of the RPF army, ordered the attack on the President's plane so that he could seize power.

President Kagame responded to Bruguiere's claims at the Kensington meeting. His anger at this latest example of French arrogance towards Rwanda erupted as he suddenly started speaking in English.

His attitude was much the same as in his interview with Fergal Keane, broadcast on BBC2's Newsnight at the end of January, when he said: 'That Judge Bruguiere says this or France says that – I don't give a damn.' He further emphasised his scorn for the Judge's attack by adding, 'Would I care that bloody Habyarimana died?'

At the London meeting the President clearly presented himself as a freedom fighter whose mission in life was to undo the wrongs of the repressive Habyarimana regime. Further French involvement in his country was unwanted. They should back off, as his Government continues the long process to rebuild Rwanda's shattered economy and society.

I support the President in his anger against the French. They have blood on their hands in Rwanda. Not only did the French prop up the Habyarimana regime, but they also trained and supplied arms to the Genocidiares. In addition their Operation Turquoise intervention, towards the end of the Genocide, allowed thousands of killers to escape to Zaire.

In autumn 2006 the Rwandan Government launched an inquiry into France's role during the Genocide. Was Bruguiere's allegation just an example of 'tit for tat' politics? It has certainly had a big impact on French influence in the country, as the Rwandan government ordered the French Ambassador and his staff to leave, shut down the French radio station and closed French schools. Rwanda has also applied to join the Commonwealth – a further demonstration of Kagame's apathy towards the French.

As reported in The Times in February, President Kagame has been invited to attend the 2007 Commonwealth summit in Uganda, as an observer. Kagame was quoted as saying, 'I hope they will then approve our membership. I am looking forward to it.'

The BBC also reported in February that Agathe Habyarimana, the former president's wife, had lost an appeal to be granted political asylum in France. Mrs Habyarimana was one of the architects of Hutu Power and has been living in France since the Genocide. Perhaps the French are offering a political olive branch to President Kagame?

Madame Habyarimana quickly responded to her failed asylum bid by launching a PR offensive. She granted an interview with Alex Duval Smith which appeared in The Observer on February 18. In the interview she positions herself as a misunderstood victim, a First Lady who spends most of her time doing charity work, only going abroad at the invitation of other First Ladies.

She strenuously denies any involvement in planning the Genocide. 'How could it have been? Can you imagine me making death lists on 6 April when I was in the garden of our Kanombe home, in darkness, picking up debris of my husband's plane that were raining from the sky? They were firing at our home. All I could do was cry and pray. My daughter Jeanne phoned the French embassy to ask them to get us out. It took the French three days.'

She then turns her anger on the RPF. 'Hutus, Tutsi and Twas all suffered because of the RPF. When they invaded in 1990, they massacred everybody. There were Tutsis in the RPF who broke away and killed Hutus and there were Hutus who killed Tutsis. Before 1990, Rwanda was in peace. I have a brother who has had four wives, three of them Tutsis. I had Tutsi friends, I still have, we phone each other.'

She is still at the top of Rwanda's 'most wanted' list – but will Madame Habyarimana's charm offensive succeed in persuading the French to change their minds and allow her to stay?

Improved relations between the UK and Rwanda have resulted in the arrest of four alleged killers who had somehow managed to find a 'sanctuary' in England following the Genocide. At the time of writing it seems likely that they will soon be deported back to Rwanda for trial. The accused men's bid to avoid extradition from Britain failed in March 2007.

Newspaper reports have speculated that a further 20 genocidaires are at large in the UK. I feel confident that finally, 13 years after the horrors of 1994, they will have to answer for their crimes against humanity.

The path to justice and reconciliation is tortuous. The fallout from the Genocide will continue to have a massive impact on the next generation. Look at what happened to me. I should be a traditional Rwandan mum surrounded by a noisy brood of children.

But that was not to be.

I thank God for Roger. He is such a happy, positive young man. I am also thankful for the opportunities that he is being given to develop and express his talents in the UK. The last 10 years have been a struggle for me. But I hope that I am about to turn a corner and become established in this exciting country.

When I went to Brussels in 2006, I was asked my nationality. I was proud to say that I am British. Thank you, Britain, for giving me the chance to live again.

Postscript to 2008 edition

The launch of Miracle in Kigali in October 2007 marked the end of the long journey to bring my story to a wider audience. Both Roger and I have been delighted with the response. The book's publication set us on another journey – talking to church groups and clubs and societies about our experiences and hopes for the future.

As I write, we are planning a visit to Rwanda in July to launch the book in Kigali. The possibility of visiting Rwanda with my book has been a long cherished dream. I would like to thank Paul Dickson, along with The Tagman Press team and Claver Gatete and Patrick Gihana Mulenga at the Embassy of Rwanda, for making this possible.

With Paul and Sally Simpson's help, we also arranged a Rwandan Genocide memorial service at Bowthorpe Church on April 5. We were very pleased that Patrick Mulenga from the Rwandan Embassy was able to join us on the day.

I am still hoping to open a Rwandan style restaurant or café in Norwich, once I have completed by catering courses at Great Yarmouth, and have gained some work experience in a hotel or restaurant kitchen.

But thanks to David Poston, a colleague of Paul's in the Royal Society of Arts Norwich group, we have started exploring the possibility of importing Fair Trade dried fruit and vegetables from a co-operative in Rwanda. If all goes to plan we should be able to involve my brother Eustache in this enterprise.

Finally we are planning to set up a Miracle in Kigali charity to help young women living in the Rwandan countryside to establish sustainable food producing businesses.

These are busy and exciting times!

Thank you very much for reading my story.

Amahoro abane namwe, Peace be with you.

Illuminée Nganemariya, April 2008

Chapter thirty three

Book Launches and Events

In the postscript to the 2008 edition, I mentioned that we were delighted with the response to the publication of this book in October 2007. But I did not explain what happened.

My brother, Eustache came over for the launch, his first trip to Europe, and stayed with me for what turned out to be a busy two weeks, with local radio, newspaper and TV interviews and a packed programme of activities.

On the journey from Heathrow to Norwich via the M25, M11 and A11, he asked 'where are all the people?' You always see people walking along the roads in the Rwandan countryside. I had to explain that it was vehicles only on British motorways!

I was so happy to have Eustache with me. He was a wonderful support as I told my story. We went to two Royal Society of Arts events, a walk at RSPB Lakenheath Fen and an early evening discussion group in Norwich, where we talked about the book. This was followed by a trip to Carrow Road to watch Norwich play Scunthorpe in the League Cup. Sadly it was a 0-0 draw, so there were no goals for Eustache.

Paul arranged for the Norwich launch of *Miracle in Kigali* to take place at the Sainsbury Centre, University of East Anglia (UEA) on the evening of 3 October. The Sainbury Centre and UEA are my favourite places in Norwich. I love walking round UEA Broad and wandering through the Sainsbury Centre's collections. It was the perfect location for my book launch.

Paul's parents and daughter Rebecca came to Norwich for the launch. It was lovely to share this special day with them. They were joined by around 150 guests, including many of the families that Roger and I had met over the years through school and football, along with staff and students from Great Yarmouth College.

Eustache, Roger, Paul, Tony Grey from our publisher, The Tagman Press and me all spoke at the launch. We had a wonderful response from our friends and other guests and spent a long time signing books, before returning home for some well deserved spicy Rwandan matoke (green bananas).

On Saturday 6 October, we headed down to Felixstowe for a book signing event at Glynis Potter's Harambee shop. It was a lovely sunny day, with lots of customers coming in to meet us. We were also able to introduce Eustache to the North Sea, an exciting experience for someone who had spent his life in a land-locked country.

Eustache's visit also coincided with my birthday, which we celebrated at Pedro's Mexican Restaurant in Chapelfield Gardens, very close to home.

The next day, we headed down to London on the train for the London launch of the book. Eustache had never been on a train, as there are no railways in Rwanda, so this was another new experience for him, which he greatly enjoyed.

The London launch was staged at Camden Irish Centre with the Rwandan Community Association. Ignatius Mugabo was our key contact. He arranged a lovely buffet featuring Rwandan and African food.

Our guest of honour was Claver Gatete, at the time Rwanda's Ambassador to the UK, who had written a foreword to the book. It was an honour to share the top table with him. He gave a very supportive and humble speech.

A reporter from BBC World Service was present and interviewed me in Kinyarwanda for their Rwandan broadcast. I was particularly pleased about this, as my family were able to hear me speak about *Miracle in Kigali* on the radio.

The evening ended with a display of Rwandan dancing, organised by Ingnatius. I was encouraged to take part. It was great fun, and a perfect way to celebrate with the Rwandan community.

The next day, we accompanied Eustache to Heathrow and bade farewell as he embarked on the long flight home with Ethiopian Airlines.

We had several more book events in the run up to Christmas at Fairhaven Woodland and Water Garden, Holy Trinity Church in Norwich, Norwich School and Great Yarmouth College. I was also interviewed for an article in the Norfolk Journal. This article was eventually to be the catalyst for Roger's acting career, but more of that later.

We began 2008 with a talk to the Norwich & District United Nations Association at the city's historic Quaker Meeting House. This was followed by an invitation to speak at the United Nations Association's regional meeting in Cambridge in February. The audience particularly appreciated Roger's talk and prophesied a great future for him.

In early March we received the exciting news that *Miracle in Kigali* was a finalist in the best factual publication category in the Creative East Awards. But before the awards evening at the end of the month, we were invited by Richard George to speak at the Cornerstone Church.

This was a very different church meeting. It began with a walk on Mulbarton Common followed by lunch and prayers in a private room at The Worlds End pub. We spoke after lunch and were greatly inspired by the clarity of the group's message.

Roger and I attended the Creative East awards evening at Norwich Theatre Royal, but it was not our night, as the winner was Poppyland Publishing. It was lovely for the book to be recognised as a finalist, an accolade that we have proudly promoted ever since.

April began with the Rwandan Genocide commemoration service at Bowthorpe Church that I mentioned in the postscript to the 2008 edition. After moving from Bowthorpe in 1997, I had kept in touch with Sally Simpson, one of the leading members of the church congregation, regularly playing badminton with her.

Sally helped arrange the service with the Rev'd Simon Stokes. Patrick Mulenga from the Rwandan Embassy made a speech and Ignatius Mugabo from the Rwandan Community Association was in attendance. We were are also very pleased to welcome the then Lord Mayor of Norwich, Roy Blower and his wife Beryl.

Simon Stokes led a very dignified service, which was attended by friends, members of the Bowthorpe Church community and a group of students from UEA. We lit candles in memory of those who had died during the Genocide and gave short testimonies.

After the service everyone stayed to talk and sample my Rwandan style spicy vegetable soup, which I had prepared the day before in the church kitchen. I was so pleased that we had all gathered again in Norwich to commemorate the Genocide.

We had more invitations in May, with a visit to London to discuss *Miracle in Kigali* at a Royal Society of Arts reading group and attendance at a service at St Edmund's Church in Taverham near Norwich.

Chapter thirty four

Off to Rwanda

In the postscript to the 2008 edition, I mentioned that we were exploring the opportunities to import Fair Trade Rwandan dried fruit and vegetables. This plan did not come to fruition. We did a lot of research, but finance was a problem.

We were also interested in setting up a *Miracle in Kigali* charity. To date we have concentrated on supporting other Rwandan focussed charities like the Glaven Valley Churches work through the Life in Abundance charity and Glynis Potter's support for Rwandan street children.

I finished my course at Great Yarmouth College in 2009 and had two catering jobs. My dream of opening my own restaurant has had to be forgotten for the moment, due to lack of money. I do, however, offer mobile catering and call myself Umuseke, which means get up early and do your work. I can create African menus with a UK twist for private dinner parties and charity and church events.

What did happen was our visit to Kigali in July 2008 for the Rwandan launch of *Miracle in Kigali*. Paul's daughter, Rebecca, joined us for the trip. It was lovely to introduce my home country to her.

With the help of the UK Rwandan Embassy, we secured a local PR and event management company called Real Innovations as our event organiser.

Juliet Mbabazi was our key contact and she arranged the launch at Hotel des Mille Collines, invited local guests and prepared our way with the media. I also contacted friends and family to ensure they came to the event. Thanks to Tony Grey, Macmillan Rwanda agreed to distribute the book for us.

Nearly 200 guests packed the main conference suite at the hotel to hear Roger, Paul and me speak. The text of my speech is included at Appendix One.

We were honoured to welcome the then Rwandan Minister of Culture, Joseph Habineza, to the event, along with former Rwandan Ambassador to the UK, Zac Nsenga, who had helped me a great deal during my early years in Norwich.

The launch was well received by the local media with coverage on Rwandan TV, several radio stations, The New Times, Izuba and The Focus. The headline in The Focus was 'A Tale of Motherly Love, or a Miracle?' The article went into the details of our story both in Rwanda and the UK. The journalist, Sam Ruburika quoted me as follows: 'If you are fighting for the truth, then the need to reconcile and forgive is imperative. Although I have never met him again, I have forgiven the murderer of my husband John.' I may have forgiven, but I will never forget.

We visited the Kigali Genocide Memorial at Gisozi to pay our respects to the many Rwandans who are buried there and also headed north to Giseyni, near the border with Congo, to visit a family of orphans supported by my friend Glynis Potter.

There was time for visits to friends and family in Kigali and we also held a big gathering for them all in our apartment.

One of the highlights of our fortnight in Rwanda was an invitation to an evening at the British Embassy, which was a short walk from where we were staying. We met many European diplomats, at what turned out to be a successful book signing event.

Back in Norwich, we spoke at the Rotary International East of England Conference in October to an audience of nearly 200 people. This was quite a daunting experience, but Paul took the audience through a powerpoint presentation and interviewed me and Roger, which helped with the nerves.

Then in April 2009 I had the honour of being invited to speak at the Rwandan Embassy's (now High Commission) Genocide Commemoration. I was very nervous giving my testimony in front of such a large gathering, but it was a memorable experience. My speech is included at Appendix Two.

In June, I was highly commended in the adult learner category in Norfolk's Big Skill Awards and received my certificate from Ray Stubbs of BBC Sport fame. This was a lovely surprise and a wonderful reward for my years of studying at Great Yarmouth College.

Meanwhile, Paul was involved in a special Christmas event at Dickleburgh Church in South Norfolk called *50 Christmas Trees in a Church*. We decided to include a *Miracle in Kigali* tree in the celebration and were able to get small Rwandan baskets from the Embassy to use as decorations.

This became an annual event for us until Christmas 2015, after which the organisers decided to take a break. We made some lovely friends, especially Reverend Norman Steer and his wife Rosemary, who were very kind to us. In 2011, we sang Rwandan carols at the launch and Norman even persuaded me to do a Rwandan dancing performance! It was a great community event and a lovely occasion.

Chapter thirty five

The Second Miracle

The phone rang in my flat on Christmas Eve 2009. It was Mark Blaney, a Producer for the British/Rwandan/South African feature film, *Africa United*. His parents-in-law live near Fakenham in Norfolk and Mark happened to be in the county for Christmas.

Africa United was five weeks from going into production and they still had not cast one of the main characters, Fabrice, a middle class teenage, Rwandan football fanatic. Mark's mother-in-law had given him an old copy of the Norfolk Journal. The magazine included the feature about *Miracle in Kigali* that I mentioned on page 127. It talked about Roger's junior football activities and there was a photograph of the two of us taken by Paul.

Mark's enthusiasm for his project was infectious and I agreed for the film's Director, Debs Gardner-Paterson to visit Norwich straight after Christmas and audition Roger in Paul's flat.

Roger picks up the story. 'I wasn't sure what was going on. Debs had a tiny hand held camera and filmed me reading some lines.'

Straight after New Year, Roger was called for a second audition in the London production office. This time he worked opposite Sherrie Silver, who already had a role in the film. 'I became aware that there was a lot of excitement about *Africa United*. We worked hard and I was really keen to get the part. But Paul told me to try and forget it, and just treat the trip as an interesting experience.'

Four days later, Jackie Sheppard, the other British Producer, called to offer Roger the role. After a flurry of administrative preparation and permissions, including voice coaching over the phone from South Africa, Roger headed to Johannesburg on 25 January – just five weeks after the initial call. This was another miracle!

'My voice coach was really impressed with my 'African' accent,' added Roger, 'but I had to work on it during filming to ensure that I used the same 'voice' throughout the two months that we were on location.'

'I was really excited on the first day of filming. It was a two-hour ride to the location, so there was plenty of time for the butterflies to grow. The first scenes that we shot involved all five of us, so we could support each other. I bonded really quickly with my fellow teenage actors and was amazed at the scale of the production – there were must have been 200 people on set.'

'The most challenging day was when we were in Johannesburg. I was so sick from the jabs that I could not get out of bed in my trailer. But I still managed to film all my scenes!'

Roger's co-stars were Yves Dusenge from Kigali, Sanyu Joanita Kintu and Eriya Ndajambaje (both from Uganda) and Sherrie Silver, who is Rwandan but like Roger had grown up in the UK.

Africa United told the story of three Rwandan children who travel 3,000 miles overland and across water, to follow their dream to take part in the opening ceremony of the 2010 World Cup. Clambering onto the wrong bus leads to their epic journey across seven countries.

Sanyu and Eriya played Aids orphans and Roger was their middle class friend, who happened to be a football prodigy. En route they met up with Yves who played a traumatised child soldier from the Congo and Sherrie whose role was a teenage sex worker in a Burundian bar.

Going back to Rwanda to work in a film was quite emotional for Roger. 'It was a strange feeling flying into Kigali without Mum. We landed at 2am and I did not expect to see any of my family. But Mum let Uncle Eustache know the arrival time and he was hiding behind a pillar in Kanombe airport. It was a lovely surprise. He was there with my eldest cousin, Mandela.'

The crew had one day in Kigali then headed north to Ruhengeri to film the

Rwandan scenes. 'Fabrice is a 'keepy-uppy' expert – I did well over 1000 'keepy-uppys' in a day. It was wonderfully rewarding to be filming there and catching up with the family.'

'Visiting Burundi was really interesting. The country is very different to Rwanda, but there is no shortage of smiling happy people. We did some amazing scenes on Lake Tanganyika and in a top class beach bar. We think that *Africa United* was the first feature film to be shot in Burundi.'

In the summer of 2010, Roger landed another role in the BBC docu-drama, *Planet of the Apemen: Battle for Earth*, which was shot in South Africa. The programme looked at the clash between Homo Erectus and Homo Sapiens.

Then on 17 October, we headed to London for *Africa United's* red carpet premiere at The Odeon Leicester Square. It was an incredibly exciting event. There was a huge bank of media with cameras and microphones all interviewing Roger and his fellow actors. The film screening was followed by a question and answer session for the actors. I was so proud of what Roger had achieved.

Roger reflected, 'If you had told me a year before that I would be involved in a film like *Africa United*, I would have laughed out loud. It was an incredible experience and it made me decide to have a go at exploring acting as a career.'

We returned to Norwich and had our own smaller premiere at The Odeon. Next on the schedule was the premiere in Kigali. The Africa United team employed me to translate the film's script into Kinyarwanda, so captions could be added to the film.

Roger flew out to Kigali in November for the premiere, where he was honoured to meet President Kagame and First Lady Jeannette Kagame at a special screening at the Serena Hotel. This was followed by a public screening at the Amahoro National Stadium.

The New Times, Rwanda's daily English newspaper gave a full report of the Serena Hotel premiere: 'The 'who is who' among the Kigali city glitterati, including top government officials, were present, as was the entire junior Rwanda football team. The event was graced by President Paul Kagame and First Lady Jeannette Kagame. The centre of the attention for the invited guests was the cast of the movie.'

'...After the screening, the cast was formally introduced to the invited guests. Roger Nsengiyumva, the star of the movie, while oozing confidence, talked about the film telling the African story from a new light.'

'However, the actor who drew a thunderous applause upon being introduced was Eriya Ndajambaje, who played the role of 'Dudu' in the hilarious film.'

'This is a new way of showing the face of Africa, the way we see and know it,' Ndajambaje said.'

It was my turn to go in front of a camera in November, when Gaile Parkin, at the time a student at MET Film School in London, filmed me for a documentary she made about Rwandans in the UK and the different ways that they have adapted to living here. Gaile knew Rwanda well and it was a pleasure to be involved in her project. She has written a well-received novel called *Baking Cakes in Kigali,* which is set six years after the Genocide.

Meanwhile, Roger secured an agent, Lindy King at United Agents, who continues to guide him as his career develops.

Chapter thirty six

Roger: Genocide Baby

Very early in January 2011, I had a call from Nick Andrews, a BBC executive based in Cardiff. He explained that he had spent many of his formative years in Kigali, where his parents were missionaries and had lived through the early days of the Genocide, before the family escaped. He was very keen to visit Norwich and discuss an idea for a documentary featuring Roger.

Nick took us for a meal at The Unthank Arms and told us that he wanted to film Roger returning to Rwanda and exploring how our home country had moved on from the Genocide. He hoped that the film would be part of a series on BBC 3 called *Extraordinary Me,* featuring young people who had had major challenges in their lives.

We were very interested in Nick's proposal and he returned to Cardiff to pitch his idea to the BBC. Nick was in touch again in matter of days to say that he had been given the go ahead for the documentary and invited us down to Cardiff to discuss the project further. The visit included a lovely evening meal at Nick's parents' house, where we met all his family.

Nick outlined the plan for the documentary. There would be some filming in Norwich in March, followed by filming in Rwanda during April. We agreed to Nick featuring excerpts from *Miracle in Kigali* in the documentary to give context to Roger's story.

Roger explains, 'I was very excited at the prospect of returning to Rwanda again and working with Nick. At the time I was into rapping and Nick agreed to try and include me rapping as part of the show. Looking back, I was very young to be confronting the issues of the Genocide by myself, including Dad's murder.

The filming process was to have a major effect on me and when I returned to the UK, I told Paul that I didn't want to talk about the Genocide again until I was 25.'

'Well it's my 25th birthday in May and I have agreed to speak about my background and my developing film career during October's Norfolk Black History Month.'

The initial filming in Norwich featured Roger and me remembering John. Then the crew went to the Open youth venue to film Roger and his friends looking at part of Fergal Keane's BBC film, about the massacre at Nyarubuye Church, during the Genocide.

Roger flew out to Kigali in early April, just as the main Genocide commemorations were beginning. The plan was for my brother Eustache to accompany Roger throughout the filming. But it was to prove emotionally very difficult for him and he only appeared in the early footage in Kigali.

Nick's fixer in Kigali arranged for Roger to meet Rwandan R & B singer Miss Jojo – Iman Uwineza. Miss Jojo suffered loss during the Genocide and she was a very good ally for him during the filming. She introduced Roger to local rappers and in the documentary there is a short piece showing him freestyling with them.

Then she went with Roger on a very harrowing journey to the church at Nyarubuye that was featured in Fergal Keane's documentary.

This was followed by an introduction to a choir that was going to sing at the main Genocide commemoration at Amohoro National Stadium. Miss Jojo and the choir invited Roger to rap as a feature within their song.

I was so proud of Roger when I saw the final documentary. There he was on stage, making his contribution to the Genocide commemorations in the packed stadium, with the President looking on.

The documentary also included a meeting between Roger and Yves Dusenge from *Africa United*. Yves is a Hutu and he and Roger met a family in the countryside and went to collect water, so Roger could experience what I had to do as a child. They talked about the past and how important it was for the new generation to work together for the future of Rwanda.

On his last day in Kigali, Roger visited a lady called Jacqueline, who had lost 12 members of her family during the Genocide and her neighbour Frederick who had been a killer. Jacqueline had forgiven Frederick, who explained that their children were growing up together.

Frederick asked Roger if he could forgive him.

After a pause, Roger said that he could forgive him, but not his father's killers.

Roger explains: 'The visit to Rwanda to film the documentary brought out an anger that I had not experienced before. My generation has a vital role to rebuild trust, but will I ever be able to forgive Dad's killers?'

Nick Andrews visited Norwich to show us the final documentary, *Roger: Genocide Baby*, before it was broadcast in July. It was an excellent programme and I am sure that it has helped Roger's generation understand what happened in 1994. I was so impressed with the way that Nick had woven in our story from *Miracle in Kigali*. He dedicated the programme to John, which was very thoughtful of him.

Nick spoke to Rowan Mantell of the Norwich Evening News just before the programme was screened: 'I saw this funky young actor on the television and recognised his name as being from Rwanda, and wondered whether this could be the film I had always wanted to make about Rwanda.'

'Initially both Roger and Illuminée were a little bit cautious. Roger carries a lot of his mum's pain, he is the only child in a single-parent family, and I felt he did this for his mum and for the wider world to know the horrors of the Genocide.'

'He was very open, and there were tears. I think we pushed him pretty much as far as he was able to go at 17. I felt very responsible for him and we spoke at length, most days, about how he was feeling.'

'There were tears, but there was also laughter. I watched the film with both Illuminée and Roger and afterwards Illuminée said it was a beautiful film. I think, not because it's beautifully shot, but because there is beauty in some of the people and the emotions, and in Roger's response to what he encounters.'

Back home, Roger landed a part in a new CBBC drama called *Postcode*. He played a Somali refugee growing up in London, who befriends a rich white boy called Zac. Three episodes were made and broadcast in December 2011, but unfortunately the show wasn't given a second season.

Earlier that summer, Fiona Rawlinson from Hereford contacted Paul. Her church, St Peter and St James had connections with Rwanda and she was keen to sell *Miracle in Kigali*. She also wanted us to come to Hereford to talk in the church and show *Africa United*.

We headed over to Hereford for the weekend at the beginning of November. Mark Blaney and Jackie Sheppard, *Africa United's* producers', gave us permission to show the film on the Saturday night. Then during the Sunday morning service, with Nick Andrews' permission, we showed excerpts from *Roger: Genocide Baby* and discussed the documentary. Fiona and her husband were very kind hosts and the church congregation gave us a wonderful welcome. We have been meaning to go back to Hereford ever since, but, as usual, time slips away.

Miracle in Kigali entered the digital world in spring 2012, when it was published worldwide as an e-book. It is very exciting to think that anyone in the world with access to a computer, tablet or smartphone can download my story and read it on their device.

The e-book launch coincided with a special event at the Revelation Christian Bookshop and Café in Norwich. Steve Foyster, a good friend of *Miracle in Kigali* and more recently Paul's book publishing business, hosted an evening called 'Hope in a Broken World' at which I spoke with Tony Grey, our original publisher. We also showed the excerpts from *Roger: Genocide Baby*.

Chapter thirty seven

Sixteen

In the summer of 2012, Roger had a meeting with film-maker Rob Brown. He had written a script about a former Congolese child soldier, who had moved to the UK and had been adopted. This was going to be Rob's first feature film and he wanted Roger to play the lead role.

This was fantastic news for Roger, being given the opportunity to play his first serious major role. His character, Jumah, had to confront the impact of his former life as a child soldier on his new life in London.

Rob and his producers were working hard to raise the funds for *Sixteen* and filming was not scheduled to take place until the following spring.

In the autumn I was asked to cook for a special CAFOD (Catholic Agency for Overseas Development) event at St John's Roman Catholic Cathedral in Norwich. CAFOD has done much good work in Rwanda since the Genocide, particularly supporting widows and helping them rebuild their lives. The event was fundraising for a new project called Connect 2 Rwanda.

I decided that I was going to give them a good taste of Rwandan cooking with my matoke (green bananas) dish and some thick spicy vegetable soup. When I first came to the UK, matoke was a rare treat, as I could only buy the bananas in London. But now, three Asian shops in Norwich sell matoke. It is a lovely comfort food to eat in the winter.

My matoke and soup were very well received at the event, as were the Rwandan Christmas cards that we had on sale along with *Miracle in Kigali*.

Sixteen was shot, as planned, in spring 2013, with Rachel Stirling playing the role of Roger's adoptive mother. Rachel also very kindly looked after Roger during the four weeks of filming in London.

Being involved with *Sixteen* helped Roger make up his mind about his next move. He wanted to be readily available for auditions, so decided that he should live in London.

I always knew the time would come when he wanted to strike out on his own, but this was going to be a major wrench. I was brave and supported him in his decision, as he searched for accommodation. Once this was secured in the Manor Park area, Roger headed off to London at the beginning of September.

Sixteen had its first screenings during the 2013 London Film Festival. We much enjoyed seeing the film at the Institute of Contemporary Arts just of The Mall. I know I am his Mum, but Roger's performance in the film was amazing. He really brought the troubled character of Jumah to life on the screen. One of the great treats that we had on the day was to meet Rachel Stirling's mum, Diana Rigg – especially for Paul, as he had seen her in TV and film roles since the 1960s.

In 2014, Roger had his first role in an ITV Drama – *Chasing Shadows,* a thriller starring Reece Sheersmith, Alex Kingston and Don Warrington and also appeared in a Norwegian thriller called *The Third Eye.*

The Third Eye was filmed in Norway and Roger played a London drug dealer up to no good in Oslo. His character met a 'sticky' end, which was a first for Roger on screen. There were dramatic moments off set as well, when Roger managed to miss his flight to Oslo, but all was well as the Norwegian production team managed to get him on another plane.

Roger was also exploring the job market in London, to help him keep going when not involved in a filming project. To begin with, he worked at a nightclub, so that he would have time for auditions during the day. But this proved too exhausting, as he could be working until 5am.

His next job was at a lovely pub in Shoreditch called The Commercial Tavern. Roger did a cocktail course before getting this job and I was very impressed with the non alcoholic cocktail that he produced for me when we visited.

The owners were supportive of Roger's acting career, but eventually he decided that agency work would be more flexible, so he initially did some shifts in packaging warehouses, before opting for labouring on building sites.

Back in Norfolk, Rosemary English, from Holy Trinity Church, introduced us to Claude and Ethne Scott. Claude had grown up in the Congo where his father was a missionary. After a visit to Rwanda and the Congo in 2010, Claude started working with the Glaven Valley Churches, on the North Norfolk Coast, to raise money to supply water purifiers in rural Rwanda.

He invited us to Blakeney, at the end of October, to show *Roger: Genocide Baby* at an evening which would also raise money for the water purifiers. We had a lovely meal at Claude and Ethne's house before heading to a packed Blakeney Methodist Church to show the film. After the film there was a question and answer session, before I signed copies of *Miracle in Kigali*.

Claude wrote a lovely report of the evening. Here's an extract: 'We were deeply moved to hear the teenager's own search for some kind of reconciliation with his father's killers and to see if he could find a way to forgive them, as indeed his mother had done. Roger took part in a national remembrance event, singing with other young people in front of thousands of people, some of them still clearly traumatised by the memory of the Genocide. All in all this was a very moving experience for all of us and gave us new and very deep insights into a nation which has made huge strides since the Genocide, but is still coming to terms with the events of 1994.'

We decided to organise a Genocide Commemoration in 2015, which was held at Chapelfield Methodist Church in Norwich on 7 April. We were joined by friends and members of the public who all lit candles in memory of those killed during the Genocide. Claude Scott was our main guest. He explained the Glaven Valley Churches' work in Rwanda and gave a demonstration to show a water purifier in action. At the end of the commemoration we had a collection for the water purifier project.

On 25 March (which had happened to be Paul's 60th birthday), we had been in London for the official premiere of Roger's film *Sixteen*. The screening was at The Lexi in Kensal Rise. This beautiful cinema is the UK's first social enterprise independent digital cinema. The day before the premiere there was a big feature, written by Liz Hoggard, about Roger and *Sixteen* in the Evening Standard.

In the feature Roger reflected on *Sixteen* and his life growing up as a Genocide survivor: 'For Nsengiyumva, it was refreshing to see an African story through a different lens. He and his mother are wary of Hollywood films about the Rwandan Genocide 'which took place in a setting Western audiences can't relate to, so they care less about it. It's good that Rob has made a film about trauma in an English environment. And we see how Jumah's trauma interacts with the Londoner's around him.' Speaking about the *Roger Genocide Baby* he said: 'I have a responsibility to speak out because my age marks exactly the time the Genocide started.'

We also had our own Norwich premiere for *Sixteen* on 21 May at Cinema City with an audience primarily made up of supportive friends.

In March 2017 *Sixteen* was recognised in the Royal Television Society West of England awards staged at the Bristol Old Vic. The film won Best Feature Film and Best Editing and Roger was a finalist in the Best On Screen Performance category.

Chapter thirty eight

Les Blancs

Tony Grey retired from publishing in 2015 and closed The Tagman Press, so Paul took on the responsibility for publishing *Miracle in Kigali*. This was the spur for him to develop his publishing business in Norwich, Paul Dickson Books, which is gradually building, focussing on Norfolk based writers.

Roger began working on his own film project in 2015, writing, producing, directing and acting in his *Avaldar (Of Ages)* trilogy – comprising three short films. Roger describes the trilogy as 'sci fi meets scripture'. He began with part two *No More Kings* and completed filming its first section – *a memory* – in 2015.

Alvadar (Of Ages) then had to be put on the 'back burner' as Roger landed his first role in a play and made his London stage debut in *Les Blancs,* at The National Theatre, in spring 2016.

Les Blancs, which is set at a mission hospital in an unspecified African country, just as the locals are about to rise up against colonial rule, dates from the 1960s. It was the work of the African-American playwright and writer, Lorraine Hansbury, who died from pancreatic cancer at the age of 34 in 1965.

Les Blancs was unfinished on her death, but Larraine Hansbury's former husband Robert Nemiroff worked on the drafts to create a production text.

Roger was given the part of Ngago, with rehearsals beginning early in the New Year. There was drama away from rehearsals, when Roger fell running up the stairs at his new home in Walthamstow and dislocated his shoulder. Intensive physiotherapy, organised by The National Theatre, ensured that he was on track for the opening of the production.

We booked tickets for one of the preview evenings and headed down to London on 22 March. I had never been to The National Theatre and was really impressed by the size of the building and the number of people heading for the various productions on the theatre's stages.

Les Blancs was in the Olivier Theatre. We had tickets near the back, but had an excellent view of the action. Unfortunately, half way through the first half, the revolving stage broke down and the play had to be abandoned for the night. Roger's main speech was in the second half, so a return visit had to be planned to see the whole play. However, all was not lost, and we enjoyed going round to the stage door where Roger met us and took us upstairs to the cast and crew bar for a drink.

Tickets were arranged for a return to London on 16 April and a matinee performance. This time we were in the second row, so were very close to the actors. As the play began, I almost felt as if I was on the stage. We were swept along by this very tense drama wondering what would happen to each individual as the story unfolded.

Roger's character was on the side of the African uprising and he made a very intense speech about his people and their rights towards the end of the play. It was incredible to see him live on stage at The National Theatre.

After the play we went to the cast and crew canteen for something to eat, then Roger took us backstage to see his changing room and also onto the set. It was a brilliant experience to stand on the stage and look out into the auditorium and think of all the famous actors who had stood where we were.

While Roger was showing us round, members of the cast came onto the stage. I recognised James Fleet from *The Vicar of Dibley* and Gary Beadle from *East Enders* and they both agreed to have a photograph with me. We also met Siân Phillips who Paul had seen in many TV and theatre productions over the years.

After *Les Blancs* closed, Roger was soon back into his routine of working and making himself available for auditions.

144

Chapter thirty nine

Informer

2017 was a busy year for Roger, he landed a role in the new *Tomb Raider* film, which was shot during the first half of the year. He played one of Lara Croft's bike courier colleagues.

Then he worked with Rob Brown again as DC Slater in *Armchair Detectives*. This BBC production was filmed in Edinburgh during the summer of 2017 and was broadcast on daytime TV during 2018.

Work on *Armchair Detectives* was swiftly followed by Roger's first major TV role as Dadir in the BBC's *Informer*. This was Roger's biggest project to date, with filming running from September through to February 2018. All of Roger's scenes were in London, so he could operate from his Walthamstow base.

At Christmas Roger told me that he was going to buy a car and move back to Norwich in the spring. He was also planning to buy a dog, but that would happen later in the year.

This was lovely news, as 2018 was to prove to be a difficult year for me. Sadly both my Mum and my half brother, Kayitani passed away. Mum had lived with my eldest sister, Berencille, for nearly 10 years, after she had broken her leg in fall at her new home. The leg did not heal well and she became bed-ridden in her final years.

I had seen Mum on return visits to Rwanda and had also kept in touch on the phone. But that became more difficult as her hearing deteriorated. Sadly, I was not able to fly out to Kigali for her funeral, but my family sent me a DVD of the service and burial which was a great help to me. But I will visit Rwanda again, before too long, so I can go to her grave and say goodbye properly.

Kayitani had suffered terribly during the Genocide. As I described earlier in the book, he had been attacked by the Interahamwe and left for dead. Mum had nursed him back to life, but he was never the same again. His wounds finally caught up with him last year, when he slipped into a coma.

Roger settled back home in Norwich on a full time basis from June and signed up with an agency to work on building sites. Having Roger living at home was a great help to me as I grieved from Mum and Kayitani. His new car meant that he could easily head down to London for auditions and meetings with his agent.

In the autumn, Roger invited me to a special screening in London of the first episode of *Informer*. He looked great on screen, playing the role of a third generation Somali immigrant and his character was very much on the edge.

There were some fabulous reviews about Roger in *Informer*. This is from Bustle. com: 'The actor's been dazzling viewers already with his role as Dadir Hassan on *Informer*. The BBC describes his character as charismatic, ebullient but a half-cocked hand grenade, any interaction with Dadir could end in a hug or a fist fight.' His onscreen dynamic with Nabhaan Rizwan aka Raza Shar is electrifying, and their growing friendship, becomes the heartbeat of the show.'

And from Tim Dowling in The Guardian ...'Shar's overnight cellmate Dadir Hassan (Roger Nsengiyumva) is particularly great in a role destined to expand over the coming weeks.'

Also Alastair McKay in the Evening Standard...'Watch out, too, for Roger Jean Nsengiyumva as the charismatic Dadir Hassan. He's a dealer, not a thief, but he steals the show.'

Tuesday evenings in front of the TV became a must, as the tense story unfolded on screen. Of course, as Roger's mum, I kept worrying that he would be safe. I knew he was acting, but I couldn't help myself!

During 2018, Roger decided to get a range of voice over show reels produced and registered with his agent's voice talent agency, United Voices. So he is now available to do commercials and also provide the voice for documentaries. This could provide an exciting new departure for him as he becomes more experienced.

In late September, Paul and I took a stall at the Afro-Caribbean Market in The

Forum, Norwich. My sister Drocelle supplied us with a selection of Rwandan crafts to sell, including our traditional baskets. We also sold *Miracle in Kigali*. The two days were a great success, as we reconnected with old friends and also made lots of new contacts.

Then Roger's puppy arrived. He had bought a very friendly, and soon to become very boisterous, Rottweiler puppy called Bo Bo. My life has been changed by Bo Bo, with very early morning trips outside, regular walks in the local area, trying to keep him entertained and feeding his voracious appetite. It can be quite exhausting, but looking after Bo Bo is very rewarding!

2019 began with Roger turning his attention again to his film project *Avaldar (Of Ages)*. He finished the script for the second part of *No More Kings*, which is set in the year 2055. Filming is planned to take place over two days in March.

Look out for the name Roger Jean Nsengiyumva. I am sure that he will go far!

Postscript to the 2019 edition

The impact of the Genocide on my mental and physical health still casts a shadow over me 25 years on.

My energy levels can be very low and post traumatic disorder is always there in the background.

I have had a lot of help and support from doctors and nurses in the NHS, for which I am eternally grateful. But sadly, sometimes that help is not consistent and can have a negative impact on my well-being.

I try to keep everything positive, but, as we all know, life can knock you down when you least expect it.

I love the Norfolk coast and countryside and going for walks. Locally my favourites are Eaton Park and University of East Anglia. A walk always calms my spirit.

I am planning another book, this time featuring my favourite recipes and hope that the process will be as rewarding as *Miracle in Kigali* has been.

Finally I would like to thank Paul and Roger for their love and support. They keep me going!

Who knows what will unfold during this year and the years to come?

Amahoro, abane namwe. Peace be with you.

Illuminée Nganemariya

Appendix One

Illuminée's Speech

Hotel des Mille Collines, Kigali, Rwanda
17 July 2008

Minister, Ladies and Gentleman

I would like you to stand up for a few moments in silence to remember those murdered in 1994.

Thank you

Why did I want to write a book?

My book is called Miracle in Kigali. If you read it you will understand that my survival with my son was a true Miracle.

Why did I want to tell my story?

It has been part of my therapy. The act of writing has helped me move on from my experiences during the Genocide.

But I also hope that by telling my story it will help others deal with the scars of 1994.

I am going to give you a flavour of my story.

I talk about growing up in a very happy family, my education, my marriage to

John, which was cut short by the Genocide and my terrifying journey through the streets of Kigali in May and June 1994 and my subsequent struggle to deal with the trauma of the Genocide and life in a foreign country.

I work hard to look forward ,even though it is not easy as a survivor.

Reconciliation is so important and I hope my book will play a small role in helping my country heal its wounds.

I would like to thank everyone in Rwanda and Britain who helped me, as I struggled to live again after 1994. I would like to thank Britain, the country that has accepted my son and me.

I would like to mention three people who worked so hard for me, my therapist Stephen Christianson, the person who made my story a reality, Paul Dickson and His Excellency Claver Gatete, Ambassador of Rwanda in the UK and his team.

But finally my heart-felt thanks go to Roger, my brother Eustache and all my family for their support, love and kindness.

Appendix Two

Illuminée's Speech

UK Rwandan Embassy's Genocide Commemoration
7 April 2009

Your Excellency Ambassador Claver Gatete, Ladies and Gentlemen.

It is 15 years since the Genocide. It sounds a long time ago, but for survivors it can seem as if it was just yesterday. What I mean is that our wounds and scars are still with us. If anything touches those scars it hurts. It reminds us of our experiences in 1994.

I was brought up in Gacuriro, Kigali, and married my husband John on 3 April 1994. We were living in Nyakabanda. I lost John on 10 May, just a few days after our son Roger was born. I, like many Rwandans, also lost members of my family and close friends.

All survivors have different stories to tell. It was a miracle, that my son and me survived in the chaos of Kigali. I was helped by Rwandans with a kind heart who hated the bloodshed.

I even joined the exodus to Zaire and possible death from cholera in a refugee camp. But was lucky to be turned back on Mount Kigali by the Rwandan Patriotic Front (RPF).

Those RPF soldiers, who appeared out of the early morning mist on Mount Kigali, will be my heroes for the rest of my life.

I moved to England in 1996 and live in Norwich with my son Roger. I would not be here, now, if it had not been for the help of many NHS doctors and nurses, who helped me through troubled times, along with the support of my family and friends.

I chose to expose myself, to be naked, in a way, and told my story in the book, Miracle in Kigali. I would like to thank my co-author Paul Dickson, and The Tagman Press for making my dream come true. I would also like to thank Ambassador Gatete for his support.

But why did I want to open myself up in this way?

It was first of all medication to help myself get better, to see if I could be healed.

Secondly it was to help ensure that what happened cannot happen again.

Thirdly to give the message of hope for the future, especially the next generation of Rwandans.

A lot has happened to Rwanda and Rwandans in the last 15 years. For we survivors it is a long journey. We try to forgive, but we will never forget. We will never be the same again, but we can keep going. We will not turn the clock back, but we can look forward.

My message to survivors is to take our time, appreciate our lives and not to be ashamed about the past, and what happened to us in 1994. It was not our fault. Try to work for a better life for you, your children and their children.

Some people say that there was no Genocide and keep saying it. But my story and me are living testimonies to the fact that the Genocide took place in 1994.

I read in the New Times that survivors have been killed who testified at a Gacaca court and that people have attacked the Gisozi memorial.

The people who do these things may think that they still have power, but they need to face their own demons, and then they can meet the angel.

Finally, my message to all Rwandans, survivors, at this difficult time of year – try to care and love yourself, be strong, have hope and move forward in your life.

Appendix Three

Rwanda: a brief history (2007 edition)

Paul Dickson

Rwanda is one of Africa's smallest nations, approximately the same size as The Netherlands. Known as 'Le Pays de Mille Collines,' land of a thousand hills, it is a beautiful, fertile country. Central Rwanda is a lush green landscape of terraced hillsides growing green and yellow bananas, sogum, cassava, mango and guava.

Unusually, a colonial cartographer's hand did not draw lines on a 19th century map to create Rwanda. Its borders were defined as much by physical characteristics as the result of expansion by the Tutsi kings, the Mwami, from the 17th century onwards.

The huge Lake Kivu to the west and the Virunga volcanoes to the north west created natural frontiers, as did the low marshland to the east, now designated as the Akagera National Park.

The borders were consolidated by the colonial powers when, at the 1885 Berlin Conference, Rwanda and its southern cousin Burundi became part of German East Africa. The British were to the north in Uganda, the Belgians to the west in the Congo, (later Zaire, and now the Democratic Republic of Congo) and the German's largest colony, Tanganyika, (now Tanzania) to the east.

The landscape protected the peoples of Rwanda from the horrors of the slave trade. It also prevented an extensive white influence until the arrival of the Belgians during World War I. The Germans had minimal impact on Rwanda.

They were present in small numbers from 1894, but governed remotely from Dar es Salaam in Tanganyika.

The first European to find his way to Rwanda was the British explorer, John Hanning Speke. What he discovered was not a tribal society, but a population split into distinct groups, which shared the same culture and language, Kinyarwanda. This was a feudal land ruled by the Tutsi Mwami with a well-ordered national, regional and local government. Each hill had its chief who in turn was answerable to a 'provincial' chief, who ultimately owed his position to the Mwami and his senior chiefs, in charge of the army, land and pastures.

The three population groupings were Hutu, Tutsi and Twa. The Twa, who comprise only 1% of the population, are thought to be the original inhabitants of Rwanda. Traditionally they were hunter-gatherers, living in more heavily wooded areas. They also became famed for making pottery. The largest group, the Hutu, around 80% of the population, were farmers living from the fruits of the land. The Tutsi, the final group, are thought to have migrated from the north during the middle ages. They were primarily pastoralists looking after cattle. But many Tutsis also lived side by side with Hutus as farmers on the hills.

This complex, well-ordered feudal land must have puzzled the early explorers. How could the Rwandans have established such control without the benefits of European education and culture? Fantasies about the origins of Rwanda's society sowed the seeds for the antipathy between Hutu and Tutsi, which culminated in the horrors of 1994.

The early Europeans viewed the Tutsis as a superior 'race', mainly based on their physical characteristics. These characteristics were by no means mutually exclusive to the Tutsis. The Europeans created a vision of the noble Tutsi, a white man in a black skin, naturally superior to the Hutu, who looked like any other central or southern African. The Twa, a pygmy people, were viewed as being at the bottom of the anthropological pile. So the tall, slender Tutsi, with their fine features and beautiful women, were deemed to be natural leaders who came from the north to civilise their Hutu and Twa 'subjects'.

But all was not as it seemed. There were Hutu provinces or principalities to the north west and south west of Rwanda that remained independent of Mwami rule until the arrival of the Belgians. The Mwami's Chief of Land was invariably a Hutu, and Hutus were well represented as chiefs at both provincial and hill level.

The Germans governed with a light hand after they arrived in 1894, using the existing Tutsi-led structures. But all this was to change in 1916, when the Germans lost their foothold to the Belgians from the neighbouring Congo. The League of Nations granted a mandate for Belgium to 'manage' Rwanda and Burundi as a unit to be known as Ruanda-Urundi. This mandate saved Rwanda from the excesses of Belgian colonial zeal, as they had to answer to the League for their actions.

The Belgians, falling in with the 'master-race' idea, implemented rule through a Tutsi elite. They felt their way for the first decade, as the Roman Catholic missionaries set about converting the country.

The colonial administrators struggled to establish a good working relationship with the Mwami, Yuhi V Musinga, who had fought alongside the Germans during World War I. He also stuck to his traditional beliefs and avoided the advances of the missionaries. In 1931, the colonial administration tired of Musinga and deposed him in favour of one of his sons, Mutara III Rudahigwa. Rudahigwa proved much more compliant, dispensed with all the rituals associated with the Mwami, and eventually converted to Roman Catholicism.

Belgian administrators came and went, but the missionaries – the only white people to speak Kinyarwanda – stayed. It was the Catholic church that was the real power behind the throne. Secondary education was almost entirely focused on the Tutsi elite, the 'natural born rulers', who quickly realised that conversion to Christianity would be a good political move. The only way for a Hutu to progress politically was to take the Catholic sacrament, aspire to become a priest and receive further education at a theological college.

Bishop Classe, who had arrived in Rwanda as a missionary at the turn of the century, encouraged the colonial administration in its policy of creating this racial divide. In 1930 he wrote, 'The greatest harm the government could possible inflict on itself and on the country would be to do away with the Mututsi caste. Such revolution would lead the country into anarchy and towards anti-European communism... As a rule, we cannot possibly have chiefs who would be better, more intelligent, active, more capable of understanding ideas of progress and even more likely to be accepted by the population than Batutsi.'

One of the Belgian's most dangerous legacies was the introduction in 1933 of an identity card, which defined the inhabitants of Rwanda in terms of race. They attempted to separate Hutus and Tutsis by physical characteristics, but gave up and split the people on economic grounds. Rwandans who owned 10 or more cattle were registered as Tutsis. Every Rwandan was required to carry a card identifying themselves as Hutu, Tutsi or Twa.

The identity card system was continued by the Hutu regimes which succeeded the Belgians in the 1960s. Cards were used to identify Tutsis in the 1963 and 1973 troubles, as well as at the Interahamwe roadblocks during the Genocide.

Tutsis gradually replaced Hutu chiefs at provincial and hill level. Many of the local Hutu chiefs became 'Tutsi' – only to change their ID cards back to Hutu in 1959 during 'the Winds of Destruction'. By the 1950s Hutu influence had effectively vanished from Rwanda's local government.

Before their departure in 1916 the Germans had established coffee as a cash crop, and under Belgian rule it upset subsistence farming on the hills. Feudal relationships were replaced with forced labour to deliver the Belgian administration's coffee. Failure to comply with forced labour requirements led to harsh reprisals meted out by the Tutsi elite on behalf of the colonial power.

In the wake of World War II, independence movements sprung up all over Africa.

Rwanda was no exception. Both Tutsi and Hutu groups lobbied Belgium for independence. The Catholic Church, having supported Tutsi domination in the 1920s and 30s, changed 'sides' after World War II and began favouring the disenfranchised Hutu majority. In The Rwanda Crisis: History of a Genocide the historian Gerard Prunier explains this volte-face as a combination of the Tutsi elite pressing for independence and a change in the social status of the priests who came to Rwanda from Belgium.

"The early leaders of the Catholic church in Rwanda such as Mgr Hirth and Mgr Classe had been upper class men with rather conservative political ideas which were followed by the rest of the white clergy. But in the late 1930s and increasingly after the war, these men were replaced by clerics of humbler social origins, from the lower middle class or even the working class and increasingly Flemish rather than Walloon. They had no sympathy for aristocratic Tutsi and identified more readily with the downtrodden Hutu."

One of the main beneficiaries of this development was Gregoire Kayibanda, a Hutu product of the Catholic seminaries. He became editor of the Catholic newspaper Kinyamateka in 1956 and gave Hutu dissidence a voice. In 1957, Kayibanda and eight other Hutu intellectuals published the Bahutu Manifesto. The manifesto was an appeal against the domination of the Tutsi 'race' and the continued isolation of Hutus from political power.

The manifesto was followed by the birth of several Hutu political parties. Kayibanda founded a party which became known as PARMEHUTU, Partie du Mouvement de l'Emancipation Hutu. The Tutsi elite responded with UNAR, Union Nationale Rwandaise. Meanwhile the Mwami, Mutara III, was poisoned in July 1959 and was replaced by his younger brother Kigeli V.

Kigeli's reign was short-lived. In November 1959, riots inspired by PARMEHUTU led to widespread burning of Tutsi houses and Tutsi murders. In what became known as the Winds of Destruction, the riots forced the first mass emigration of Tutsis to neighbouring countries. Kigeli V departed, never to return.

The Belgian colonial administration, which by now had swapped sides to favour the new Hutu parties, stood by and watched the attacks on Tutsis. With the Mwami and his court and the traditional power structures effectively terminated, the Belgians organised elections. In 1961 PARMEHUTU swept to power with a massive majority, with UNAR only managing to gain handful of seats.

With Belgian help, Kayibanda declared Rwanda a republic on January 28, 1961, forestalling any possible intervention by the United Nations (Rwanda was still under UN mandate, a legal position inherited from the League of Nations at the end of World War II). The declaration of the republic was followed by more attacks on Tutsis and a further flood of exiles. It was in 1961 that the parents of Rwanda's current President, Paul Kagame, left Gitarama with their young son and headed for exile in Uganda. From the start, the killing sprees combined assaults on both the elite and ordinary Tutsis on the hills. Tutsi families who remained in Rwanda learned to live with the constant threat of violence.

Rwanda was formally declared independent on July 1, 1962, with Gregoire Kayibanda as President. The country was split from Burundi, which remained under Tutsi control. Tutsi exiles launched an invasion from Burundi in December 1963, only to be repulsed by Kayibanda's army. Several thousand indigenous Tutsis were killed in reprisals along with all surviving Tutsi politicians. Kayibanda's regime introduced a quota system based on the proportion of Hutu and Tutsi in the population. Progress to secondary and tertiary education and to the civil service was controlled by 'ethnic' grouping rather than merit.

In 1972, the Tutsi government in Burundi orchestrated the murder of 150,000 Burundian Hutus. Kayibanda's response was a clamp-down on the quota system, leading to more Tutsi migrations to neighbouring countries.

Kayibanda was deposed in a bloodless military coup on July 5, 1973, led by Major-General Juvenal Habyarimana. Habyarimana grew up in Gisenyi, one of the Rwandan principalities controlled by Hutus until the 1920s. It remained anti-royalist throughout the colonial regime. The men from the north took over in 1973, pushing aside Hutu power blocks from the middle and south of the country.

Juvenal Habyarimana had been studying medicine in Kinshasa when PARMEHUTU swept to power, but halted his studies to join the army. He rose rapidly in the army and, in 1965, aged 28, was appointed to Kayibanda's Cabinet as Minister of the Armed Forces and the Police. Habyarimana, controlling both the army and the police, was in the ideal position to depose his former mentor. Both Tutsis and Hutus welcomed his new regime. One of Habyarimana's earliest pronouncements was to guarantee Tutsi safety.

Even though the quota system remained, Rwanda settled into a period of stability. Wealthy Tutsi businessmen became the norm; It was acceptable for Tutsis to make money so long as they did not aspire to political power.

In 1974, Habyarimana, who had banned political parties when he came to power, established the MRND (Mouvement Revolutionnaire National pour le Développement). Rwanda became a single party state; all Rwandans had to be MRND members by law. Habyarimana was the only candidate at presidential elections in 1978, 1983 and 1998.

To the outside world, Rwanda, by African standards, was a deeply religious, well-ordered nation. Opponents to the regime disappeared every now and then, but that was to be 'expected'. Western aid, particularly from Belgium and France, supported Habyarimana's regime. The political reality was very different. The Gisenyi 'mafia' ran the country for their benefit as a totalitarian state.

Throughout his 21 years in power, Habyarimana failed to get to grips with the Tutsi refugee problem. He used the exponential growth of Rwanda's population – which, despite Tutsi migrations, was tipping the eight million mark – as an excuse. Rwanda was now the most densely populated country in sub-Saharan Africa.

In the late 1980s, the world collapse in coffee prices threatened the stability of the Rwandan economy. Coffee was the country's number one cash crop. The Government blamed the old Mwami regime for the country's economic problems and began whipping up anti-Tutsi sentiment. The World Bank stepped in to help restructure the economy, but aid came at a price. Habyarimana had to introduce multi-party politics.

This threatened the Giseyni 'mafia's' control of the country. Habyarimana's wife, Agathe, was prominent in the 'mafia'. A Hutu princess, she left her mark on late 1980s and early 1990s Rwandan politics as a kind of Lady Macbeth figure. Supported by her brothers, she became the force behind 'Hutu Power' politics.

In July 1990, Habyarimana announced that the ban on political parties would be removed. This announcement was the signal for the nascent Rwandan Patriotic Front (RPF) to plan its move. The RPF comprised a core of mainly Tutsi officers and NCOs in the Ugandan Army, who were the sons of Tutsi émigrés. They had fought for President Museveni in his National Resistance Army, which toppled Milton Obote's regime in 1985. But the RPF also attracted Hutus dismayed by Habyarimana's regime.

Led by Major-General Fred Rwigyema, a former Ugandan Army Commander-in-Chief, the RPF deserted from the Ugandan army overnight, 'borrowing' equipment on the way. Rwigyema's Head of Intelligence, Major Paul Kagame, missed the moonlight flit as he was on a training course in the USA.

The RPF invaded Rwanda on October 1, 1990. But two days into the campaign, Rwigyema was killed. After early successes against Habyarimana's Forces Armée Rwandaise (FAR), the RPF was forced to flee, mainly due to French military muscle rapidly deployed in support of FAR. Paul Kagame succeeded Fred Rwigeyma and reverted to guerrilla warfare, initially from the mountainous area to the north west of Rwanda. Meanwhile, the Government's response to the invasion was to round up prominent Tutsis and anti-MRND Hutus who were imprisoned in barbaric conditions.

159

In early June 1991 a new constitution was created allowing for political parties to legally exist and, in the spirit of this new 'liberal' era, the MRND added an extra 'D' for Democratie to its name. A rash of new political parties was born. Among them was the MDR (Mouvement Democratique Rwandaise), which had at its core Hutus from President Kayibanda's old Gitarama heartland, opposed to Habyarimana's Gisenyi clique. Then there was the PL (Parti Liberal) which comprised Tutsis and moderate Hutus, and the Parti Social Democratie, an opposition party that mainly appealed to professionals.

The most dangerous 'birth' was that of the CDR (Coalition pour la Defense de la Republique). This radical Hutu party, created in 1992, spawned Radio-Television Libre Mille Collines (RTLMC) and the newspaper Kangura. Both media organs pumped out a diet of racist vitriol. The message was simple. Hutus had to watch out as the RPF, the Inyenzi (cockroaches) wanted a return to the bad old days of the Mwami. Tutsis could not be trusted, as they were probably in league with the rebels.

Meanwhile the RPF continued to mount a guerrilla campaign, boosted by a steady flow of young Tutsis and Hutus disillusioned with Habyarimana's government. The rural Hutu population, however, never greeted the rebels as conquering heroes. Thousands fled from border villages, creating a large internal refugee problem. At the same time, Hutu extremists embarked on regular killings of small groups of Tutsis, particularly in the Gisenyi and Ruhengeri Hutu heartland.

In the summer of 1992, the MDR, PSD and PL, tiring of the killings and the impact of the guerrilla warfare on Rwanda's fragile economy, met the RPF for an initial round of peace talks. This led to a ceasefire and the beginning of the main Arusha (Tanzania) peace talks, which were to last until late summer 1993.

One of the results of the peace talks was a further radicalisation of 'Hutu Power' politics and the birth of militia groups sponsored by the MRNDD and the CDR, to protect Hutu rights. The militia groups were known as the Interahamwe ('those who work together'). They were to become the shock troops of the Genocide. The French, who provided constant military support to the Government during the early 1990s, were involved in training the militias.

President Habyarimana, playing the political middle game of the Arusha peace talks, was in a dangerous position. A coup, possibly even led by his wife and her brothers, became more likely as the talks dragged on. The RPF's legal status as a political party and a seat in government was the key issue on the agenda.

In January 1993 Interahamwe militias, inspired by the CDR, launched a series of violent demonstrations which ended in Tutsi deaths. The RPF responded by breaking the ceasefire and launching an attack in the Byumba province (north east Rwanda). They advanced rapidly into Ruhengeri to the west and south to Kigali.

The RPF was guilty of civilian atrocities in Ruhengeri, giving the CDR more ammunition for its calls to root out the Inyenzi. Then the RPF declared a ceasefire with its soldiers just 15 miles from Kigali. Kagame realised that the French were lining up again to bolster the failing FAR, and thus avoided a bloody battle for the capital.

But the RPF ceasefire did not halt the growth of 'Hutu Power' politics with the CDR in the vanguard, increasingly supported by Madame Habyarimana and her brothers and a rag-bag of Hutu supremacists from other parties. Their public mouthpiece was Radio Television Libres des Mille Collines, which pumped out increasingly violent anti-Tutsi broadcasts, combined with a diet of printed hate served up by the newspaper Kangura.

The extremists continued to fight a propaganda war, blaming all Tutsis for the collapsing economy. 'Root them out and all will be well' was the message. If Hutus did not do that, the RPF 'inyenzi' would massacre the Hutu.

The Arusha peace agreement, allowing for a broad-based coalition government including the RPF, was signed on August 4 1993. President Habyarimana put his name to a document which, in hindsight, was the death warrant for more than 800,000 Rwandans.

Arusha also allowed for the RPF to be integrated with FAR. An RPF contingent was moved to Kigali to protect RPF politicians and make a start to the integration process. A small United Nations force was flown into Rwanda to monitor both the military and political process. Known as UNAMIR, United Nations Assistance Mission for Rwanda, it was headed by the Canadian General Romeo Dallaire.

Then disaster struck. In November, extremist Tutsi army officers murdered President Ndadaye, Hutu president of Burundi. The result was more bloodshed in Rwanda, with Interahamwe militias gunning down Tutsis thought to have links with the RPF.

The early months of 1994 were chaotic. No progress was made with launching the power-sharing government. The RPF politicians left Kigali, totally frustrated with the situation. Meanwhile 'Hutu Power' extremists armed the Interahamwe in secret.

On April 6, President Habyarimana flew to Arusha for a meeting about the Rwandan situation with neighbouring heads of state. He arranged to fly Burundian President Cyprien Ntaryamira home in his private Falcon 50 jet (a gift from French president Francois Mitterand). The plan was to fly to Kigali first, then take Ntaryamira on to the Burundian capital, Bujumbura. But as the plane came into land in Kigali at 8.30pm on April 6 it was shot down by surface to air missiles, and the two presidents were killed.

Who fired the missile? At the time, Hutu Power media claimed it had been shot down on orders from Paul Kagame, while others accused the militant Hutus from within Habyarimana's party of orchestrating the crash in order to provoke anti-Tutsi outrage, while simultaneously seizing power. The finger was pointed at the CDR and even Madame Habyarimana's clique. The debate continues to rage, and it is unlikely that the mystery will ever be solved, although President Kagame has gone on record to say that he would co-operate with an independent tribunal.

RTLMC immediately broadcast the news of the President's death, blamed the RPF and called for Hutus to do their work and rid the country of the Tutsi 'inyenzi'. As the radio station whipped up Hutu 'patriotic' fervour, the Presidential Guard started the killing, armed with lists of well-connected Tutsis and moderate Hutus. The Prime Minister, Agathe Uwilingiyimana, was one of the first people to be targeted along with the 10 Belgian UN soldiers who were protecting her.

The killings rapidly picked up pace. Each local Hutu Bourgmestre (Mayor) had his own list of key Tutsis and began his 'work'. The RPF quickly mobilised and advanced towards Kigali as the country descended into chaos. With the RPF on the move, RTLMC broadcasts became more and more hysterical, encouraging Hutus to kill or be killed by the cockroaches. Interahamwe roadblocks sprang up all over Rwanda. A Tutsi ID card became an instant death sentence as friend murdered friend, colleague murdered colleague and even husbands murdered wives. For the next three months, marauding Interahamwe militia roamed the countryside hunting Tutsis. Some 800,000 Tutsis and moderate Hutus were hunted down and slaughtered. There was no hiding place.

Two weeks after the Genocide began, RTLMC and the government radio station made cynical broadcasts encouraging Tutsis to come out of hiding. It was the RPF that the Interahamwe was after, they said, not ordinary citizens. Many people returned home, only to be welcomed by machete blades.

At first General Dallaire, head of the UN peacekeeping force, thought that he was in the middle of a bloody coup. He made vain attempts to broker a ceasefire between the FAR and RPF. But soon the scale of the killings made Dallaire realise that this was more than a coup. His pleas to the UN for power to intervene fell on deaf ears. As a result, his tiny UNAMIR force became an impotent bystander as the Genocide unfolded.

The French made a brief appearance on April 8 to remove French nationals along with Madame Habyarimana, her brothers and other cronies. Loyal Tutsi embassy staff were left to fend for themselves – there was no room for them on the French flights out of Kigali.

The West largely ignored the Rwandan Genocide until it was too late, wrongly branding the killings as a local tribal violence. But media reports gradually forced Western leaders to realise that this was much more than a local incident. Reporting on July 5 1994 from Kibuye in western Rwanda, the Guardian journalist Chris McGreal painted a horrific picture of the 'successful' Interahamwe campaign. Ordinary Hutus in a church congregation denied that anything had happened to their Tutsi neighbours.

"There is no shortage of evidence of what happened at the church, only an unwillingness to admit it. The bullet holes speckling the corrugated iron roof shattered windows and chipped walls, the bloody handprint of a dying Tutsi – perhaps once a member of the congregation, the thin metal toilet door sliced through by a machete in search of a victim: all testify to the murder of 3,000 Tutsis at the church on a single day in April."

"Even the Tutsi priest was killed. As if that were not enough, limbs stick out of the shallow graves sloping from the church. A skull and backbone lie on the soil, probably dragged from the grave and picked clean by dogs... But the smell of rotting flesh is the most overpowering evidence... The service made no mention of the massacre at the church and at a nearby stadium, in which almost all the town's 10,000 Tutsis were slaughtered. There was no remembrance of the victims, no plea for forgiveness. There was only denial and lies."

July 5 was the day after Kigali fell to the RPF. By then, a mass Hutu exodus had begun across the border into Zaire. The church congregation described by Chris McGreal was obviously terrified. Surrounded by the overpowering evidence of the killings, they feared for their lives, anticipating RPF revenge killings.

On June 23, the French Government, with UN support, had sent a 5,000 strong military force to south west Rwanda. This humanitarian mission, Operation Turquoise, was sent to protect surviving Tutsis. However it was welcomed with open arms by Hutu killers. The French mission did help Tutsis, but it also facilitated the flight of 'Hutu Power' politicians and thousands of Interahamwe 'soldiers'.

The Interahamwe militias were attracted to the French zone like bees to honey. Safely behind French lines, the leaders of the Genocide began their final propaganda war. The message passed to ordinary Hutus was that the RPF would descend on their villages and kill indiscriminately. The safest thing to do was to flee to Zaire.

Whole villages uprooted themselves and headed west, led by their Bourgmestres. The RPF held back from possible conflict with the French and concentrated on moving north west from Kigali to Gisenyi, the last FAR stronghold on the border with Zaire. A vast tide of humanity fled from Kigali in front of the RPF. When Gisenyi fell on July 18, some two million people had crossed into Zaire.

This is how Chris McGreal described the scene in Gisenyi in The Guardian of July 19.

"First came a single mortar among many fired as the RPF moved in to take Giseyni...It ripped into the exhausted refugees crowded onto a patch of open ground beside the border post. The shrapnel split open children's skulls, severed their parents limbs and disembowelled their friends... But the damp thud and searing chunks of metal heralded the stampede."

The scene was set for the next horrific chapter of death and destruction.

Hundreds of thousands of refugees spilled onto the hard volcanic rock on the plains of Goma, just over the border in Zaire. With no water, food, cover or sanitation, cholera and dysentery swept through the refugee camps and killed thousands.

It was then that the West finally woke up to Rwanda. A massive humanitarian operation was launched. But all it managed to do was play into the hands of the Interahamwe, who controlled the hastily established camps and became the arbiters of life and death for their fellow Hutus.

Cynically, the refugee 'Hutu Power' leaders tried to label the catastrophe in Goma as a second Genocide. But would the mass exodus have taken place if the Hutu Bourgmestres had not marched their fellow villagers to the Zaire border like latter-day Pied Pipers? The RPF came to power with messages of unity and conciliation, promising to root out those responsible for the Genocide, and assuring the safety of ordinary Hutus. That there were revenge killings at the local level is without question, but the RPF apocalypse promised by the Bourgmestres never materialised.

The new government sworn in on July 19 was headed by President Pasteur Bizimungu, a Hutu who had been the political 'voice' of the RPF. Army leader Paul Kagame was made vice president. From the start, the RPF-dominated regime featured Hutus alongside Tutsis in leading positions to promote a unified approach.

But the RPF had a huge mountain to climb. The exchequer was bare – the 'Hutu Power' government had emptied the banks. The economy was at a standstill. For the last 100-plus days the main focus had been killing, not coffee production. Hospitals had been ransacked and burned down, and there was no effective medical care. The Genocide had ripped the heart and soul out of Rwanda.

The country also had to come to terms with a massive refugee problem. Not only were there thousands of displaced Tutsi survivors in the country, but there were also many homeless Hutus who had fled in the face of the RPF. Added to that was a mass influx of Tutsi refugees returning from Burundi, Tanzania, Uganda and Zaire.

The 'Hutu Power' leaders soon managed to organise themselves in the Goma camps and embarked on raids into Rwanda, supported by President

Mobutu of Zaire, who had been a close friend of Habyarimana. Then in 1995 the Interahamwe, aided by Zairian forces, took the hate campaign to Zaire by attacking local Tutsis in South Kivu province.

The Rwandan Government tried to encourage refugees to return home from Zaire. But anyone making a move to go was likely to be killed by the Interahamwe. So in August 1996, the Rwandan Army invaded Zaire to shut down the camps, drive out the Interahamwe and enable the refugees to return home.

The following year, Rwandan and Ugandan-backed rebels led by Laurent Kabila deposed President Mobutu. The RPF hoped that this would bring an end to Interahamwe influence, but this was not to be. The Interahamwe lived to fight another day. Hutu extremist forces still lurk in Zaire to this day, supported by the Hutu diaspora.

A UN-sponsored criminal tribunal began work in Arusha, Tanzania, in 1996 to try the leading perpetrators of the Genocide. Its long drawn out proceedings are scheduled to end in 2008.

But what of the foot soldiers of the Genocide, Hutu farmers swept into the killings who enthusiastically set about destroying their friends and neighbours? A staggering 700,000 people are thought to have been involved. Rwandan prisons were soon bursting at the seams as the Government tried to deal with the fallout from the Genocide. How could a justice system cope with thousands of alleged criminals?

The Government's solution was to empower the Gacaca (meaning 'on the grass') system of local village courts to deal with lowly Interahamwe, in which elected lay judges would hear witness testimony from villagers. The path towards reconciliation, however, is strewn with difficulties. The Government no longer talks in terms of Hutu and Tutsi; only of Rwandans. But memories of the Genocide are still raw, and its impact will continue to be felt for years to come, as Aids claims its victims, a lasting legacy of the Interahamwe.

At the political level, Pasteur Bizimungu resigned as President in 2000, following the introduction of the new constitution, to be replaced by Paul Kagame. Kagame was elected President in 2003, in the first multi-party elections since the Genocide. The RPF won a landslide victory in the first parliamentary elections, also in 2003.

Since 2003, the RPF has pursued a policy of releasing prisoners back into the community to solve overcrowding problems, and is currently considering repealing the death sentence. This will ease the extradition of suspected genocidaires from countries like Britain.

Speculation over the death of Habyarimana continues to dog the RPF. Last October French Judge Bruguiere alleged that President Kagame was responsible for ordering the attack. Kagame's response was swift. Tiring of France's continued attempts to retain influence in Rwanda, he ordered the French Ambassador to leave and closed the French Embassy, radio station and schools.

Rwanda, with nearly a century of Francophone ties, has also demonstrated its antipathy to France by applying to join the Commonwealth. There is a real prospect that President Kagame will be photographed meeting HM The Queen at November 2007's Commonwealth summit in Uganda.

But will the RPF succeed in banishing Rwanda's racist politics once and for all? Only time will tell if this tiny African country, still one of the poorest in the world, can continue to plot a steady course away from the nightmare of 1994.

Paul Dickson
February 2007

Appendix Four

Glaven Valley Churches North Norfolk

Working with Life in Abundance Charity in Rwanda

'Claude, how would you like to come to Rwanda?' That apparently casual invitation from a friend came in the summer of 2009. I didn't know exactly what I was committing to, but I readily said: 'yes'. In 2010 Ethne and I went to Rwanda with a group from Southover Church in Lewes. Their aim was to work alongside Rwandans helping them in their struggle to come to terms with the after-effects of the 1994 genocide. We were moved by what we saw and the stories we heard from genocide victims, and by what was being done to help them, that we decided to go out again. And again. And again. But on these later occasions, it was with groups of people from the Glaven Valley churches in North Norfolk. They had heard us talk about our visits and wanted to go out themselves!

We have just come back from our fourth visit to Rwanda. It is 25 years since the Genocide, but we found a continuing need to engage and support people who have suffered, and still suffer from the impact of that Genocide. Our efforts now were being mediated through the work of Life in Abundance (LiA), an international charity founded by Dr Florence Muindi, a Kenyan doctor. Their over-riding philosophy is, by working through local churches, to empower others so that they can become resilient and self-reliant, able to support themselves and their families economically and to understand how to live healthy and socially beneficial lives. Their four principal areas of work are: Economic Empowerment, Community Health, Social Engagement and Education. We were very impressed to see what LiA was achieving, not just with Genocide victims, but with a wide range of people. It was a privilege to work alongside them.

Over the years, we have received huge financial support locally. This has enabled us to buy and take over water filters and also to build houses for Genocide victims, all women. Whilst doing this, we have cemented links with pastors from the Democratic Republic of Congo (DRC), where Claude lived as a child with his missionary parents.

On the 2019 trip, we took out 10 boxes of water filters – enough to provide safe drinking water to 5000 people. Most of these went to the Congo where the need is desperate. We made provision for, and helped in the building of a house for a lady who has suffered as a result of the Genocide. We provided her with furniture and a water harvesting system. We visited two women who were living in houses we had previously provided for them in 2015 and 2017. Their lives had been totally transformed. They looked really healthy and were clearly self-sufficient.

We visited a number of people who have successfully taken part in the micro-business project run by LiA. It has changed their lives. Their main source of pride was that they were now able to feed their family and send their children to school. We visited a similar project on Nkombo Island, a very poor community. Here we saw a similar project focused on people with disabilities. From being labelled 'broken pots' and deemed useless by others, they have found friendship and the encouragement to use what skills they have to earn money to support themselves.

We ran a two-day training course for Sunday School teachers so that they could help children learn Bible stories by acting them out. This involved the teachers writing Bible stories in their own words. Through this whole process, they also learned to train other adults. All 20 of them entered wholeheartedly into the activities. Their energy and enthusiasm were boundless. Unusually, all 20 of them stayed right through the whole programme! LiA will monitor how they use their learning.

On each trip, we visit Nutrition Clinics focused on children with malnutrition. We noticed that, now, under the guidance of LiA, adults were taught about a balanced diet and were asked to bring some food towards the meal given to children.

On all of our trips, we come back humbled and chastened by what we have experienced. We just love Rwanda and its people, their welcome and their generosity. The ones we met were mostly poor but always joyful in their expression of their faith. We were told over and over again that what they appreciated more than anything else was that we had come all that way to be with them and share time with them. This meant much more than anything we had brought for them.

The Glaven Valley churches now have strong links with Rwanda, which we will continue to maintain.

For more information see
www.africaglavenmission.wordpress.com
www.lifeinabundance.org

Ethne and Claude Scott
February 2019

Glaven Valley Churches volunteers set to work house building in Rwanda.

Training Sunday School teachers.

Glossary of abbreviations

CDR — Coalition pour la Défense de la République (Hutu extremist party)

FAR — Forces Armée Rwandaise (President Habyarimana's army)

FDLR — Forces Démocratique de Liberation du Rwanda (post-Genocide Hutu extremist rebels)

Interahamwe — 'Those who work together'. Hutu paramilitary organisation, the foot soldiers of the Genocide

MDR — Mouvement Démocratique Républicain (the main opposition party formed when Habyarimana legalised multi-party politics)

MRND(D) — Mouvement Révolutionnaire National pour le Développement (et la Démocratie). (Habyarimana's governing party. The second D for Démocratie was added when multi-party politics were established in the years immediately preceding the Genocide)

PL — Parti Libéral (a pre-Genocide opposition party which had Tutsi members)

PARMEHUTU — Parti du Mouvement de l'Emancipation Hutu (President Kayibanda's Hutu party formed in the late 1950s)

PSD — Parti Social Démocrate (second largest pre-Genocide opposition party)

RPF — Rwandan Patriotic Front (the mainly Tutsi-led rebel army and political organisation that is now the governing party of Rwanda)

RTLMC   Radio Télévision Libre des Mille Collines(Hutu extremist
        radio station established in 1993)

UNAMIR   United Nations Assistance Mission for Rwanda, headed by
        Canadian Lt. General Roméo Dallaire.

UNAR   Union National Rwandaise (short-lived Tutsi party formed
        in the late 1950s)

Further Reading

Shake Hands With The Devil, the Failure of Humanity in Rwanda. Lt. Gen. Roméo Dallaire – Random House

We wish to inform you that tomorrow we will be killed by our families. Philip Gourevitch – Picador

The Rwanda Crisis, History of a Genocide. Gérard Prunier – Hurst & Company

We Survived Genocide in Rwanda, 28 Personal Testimonies – Quill Press

BBC Rwanda news: bbc.co.uk/news/topics/cwlw3xz0zdet/rwanda

The Guardian Rwanda news: theguardian.com/world/rwanda

Africa news website: allafrica.com/rwanda

Rwanda High Commission London: hrwandahc.org

Miracle in Kigali blog: miracleinkigali.blogspot.com

Roger: Genocide Baby: bbc.co.uk/programmes/b012lttt

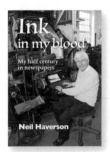

Paul Dickson Books

Books by Norfolk writers published in Norwich

Paul has lived and worked in Norfolk for the past 30 years, initially for the National Trust and, for the last 20 years, as an independent PR practitioner and latterly as an independent publisher and tour guide.

A meeting with Illuminée Nganemariya in 2006 saw Paul assisting with Miracle in Kigali, Illuminée's story of survival during the Rwandan Genocide and subsequent life in Norwich.

After a spell as a director of Norfolk's Tagman Press, Paul decided to branch out on his own. Since then he has embarked on collaborations with Norfolk writers Tony Ashman, Sandra Derry, Neil Haverson and Peter Sargent.

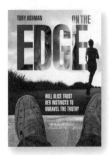
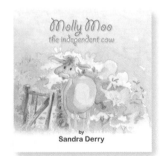

www.pauldicksonbooks.co.uk

174

Miracle in Kigali Reviews

"*Reading about real-life atrocity is never going to be something to enjoy, but it doesn't stop you from being glad you read it.*" Emma Delf Urbane magazine

"*Illuminée still cannot explain how she and her son Roger survived. Reading her book, it becomes clear that there were many, many, miracles.*" Rowan Mantell, Norwich Evening News

"*Journey of Hope, Illuminée Nganemariya survived the Rwandan Genocide to escape to a new life in Norwich with her son.*" Louise Cummings, Norfolk Journal

"*I can't say I was delighted at the prospect of reading a survivor's account of the Rwandan Genocide, but from the opening pages, Illuminée Nganemariya's modestly told narrative compels you to follow her bloody journey through Le Pays des Mille Collines--Rwanda, land of a thousand hills.*" Louisa Sutton, Cambridge Student magazine

"*Miracle in Kigali is an extraordinary document - a unique, tragic, insider's guide to Genocide. This is a book about what a mother will endure to keep her child alive. I read it and wanted to give Illuminée a big hug. She's my hero.*' Nick Andrews, BBC

Finalist Best Factual Publication, Creative East Awards 2008.